LET ME LEAD YOUR WAY

THE FINEST GUIDE TO COACHING LEADERSHIP

ELVIN COACHES

CONTENTS

Just for you!

Scan the QR code to subscribe or follow the link
https://elvinlifecoaches.activehosted.com/f/3

You're going to receive the

Wheel of Life Coaching Technique

and other goodies

INTRODUCTION

Think about a few times in your past where you worked in a group setting. This could have been for work, school, an organization, a sports team, or any other situation where you had to associate with others closely. Inevitably, these groups had someone leading the charge, whether they were appointed the position or somehow fell into it unofficially. I want you to recall these "leaders" and try to understand their role and how they fulfilled it. Were they the type who worked alongside those whom they led, encouraging them every step of the way, or did they simply stand back and try to rule with an iron fist? Perhaps they did not lead at all and were absent most of the time.

The point here is that leaders have certain unique characteristics, even though they come from a variety of backgrounds. Leaders are not always cookie-cutter in their approach, either. They all have their own strengths and talents that they bring to the table. Also, they have certain viewpoints that may or may not skew their decision-making. In the end, no matter their backgrounds, leaders have a common goal of influencing the social process and achieving specific results for a team.

One of the most accurate images out there shows the difference between a boss and a leader. The boss is standing on top of a large wagon, ordering his followers to pull. On the other hand, the leader is out in front of his followers pulling the wagon with them. Essentially, he is leading by example and has his team members' backs.

Leadership is an essential quality to possess because the world needs it. If we did not have leaders during the most pivotal times throughout history, the world would be a vastly different place. Dare I say, a scarier place. Through the toughest times, when real change needed to be made, it was a handful of individuals that stepped up to the plate and led the charge. These people were not born extraordinary, but they did extraordinary things. They were regular people who had courage and unique talents that they weren't afraid to use.

The people who succeed in different areas of their lives, whether it be work, education, family, health, relationships, etc., have a strong ability to be a leader. They can lead others as well as themselves.

But those of you reading this book are probably confused about what a leader is. You may have never been taught leadership skills or spent too much time around pseudo-leaders. Many of you may have no direction in life and are completely unaware of what to do next. These shortcomings may have resulted in many painful moments in your life where you were taken advantage of, led astray, or missed out on important opportunities. As a result, you became stuck in circumstances that you hated and always lived below your potential.

Well, it's time to get out of this rut and start living the life you deserve. We understand the struggle you have been through and want to help. If you are someone who wants to develop more leadership skills that will result in higher success rates, then you have come to the right place. Furthermore, if you have aspirations of becoming a leadership coach, whether you are already in the life coaching field or not, you have also come to the right place. In this book, *Let Me Lead Your Way: The Finest Guide to Coaching Leadership*, we will take a deep dive into the world of leadership coaching and go into great detail about what it entails and how it can benefit your life, both as a coach and client.

As you read through the following chapters, you will receive a foundational understanding of the leadership coaching field. This includes the essential qualities of being a true leader. Just like in our previous books, which covered general life coaching and business coaching, we will uncover the many techniques involved in being a leadership coach, including what types of questions to ask, how to motivate your clients to be the best, and developing the skills and methods to become the best coach and/or leader you can be.

While it's true that some individuals are born with certain qualities that give them an advantage, we can each learn how to be a good leader, both through gained knowledge and experience. With each chapter, we will bring out more detail about leadership and leadership coaching that will take you to a higher level in both life and your coaching practice. We worked hard to leave no stone unturned so that you will have a strong foundation to start improving your circumstances for the better. The first step is learning the benefits of leadership coaching. From there, if you decide to become a coach, that's the icing on the cake.

Unfortunately, so much of our training and education is spent learning various skills and information, which is often directed towards specific industries. While these are important, many essential skills that are beneficial across the spectrum, like leadership, are woefully ignored. We are here to change that with this book. Let's get started!

Leadership

WHO ARE WE?

We are collectively known as Elvin Coaches, a group of life coaches with a variety of backgrounds, experience, knowledge, and specialties. We are passionate about helping people in different areas of their lives, and we have been doing so for many years.

We met several years ago while on a retreat in Bali, Indonesia. Many of us were already in the coaching profession, and this common interest brought us all together. After working with each other for so long, we have become like a close-knit family who loves spending time together. Furthermore, we continue to learn from each other, which constantly makes us better coaches.

We have helped a number of clients over the years and several of them have become coaches themselves. We always love bringing people into the life coaching family, no matter what specialty they decide to go into. In addition, we enjoy watching people experience and understand the benefits that coaching provides. So, whether you plan on becoming a coach or not, we are pleased that you are joining us. These are the main reasons we chose to write books on the subject matter.

There are only so many people we can help with one-on-one or group coaching sessions. We wanted to introduce the concept of life coaching and the many forms it comes in to as many people as possible. We have already written two previous books, both of which contain a wealth of information. We expect our book on leadership coaching to continue our success in reaching out to those who will fall in love with the life coaching profession.

At Elvin Coaches, we support each other every step of the way. We truly believe that we are only as strong as our weakest link, which is why we are happy to work as a team. We view our clients in the same manner. Our goal is always to make sure they are in a better state after they have worked with us than they were before. We feel the same way about all of you, the readers of this book, and thank you immensely for joining us on another journey as we explore the world of leadership coaching.

1

THE BASICS OF LEADERSHIP COACHING

I n the first book of our series, *Don't Make Me Use My Life Coach Voice,* we mentioned that life coaching has many different subsets, like business coaching, which was discussed in our second book. Our focus here will be another subset in the field, which is leadership coaching. Before we continue, let's revisit some of the essential points of general life coaching.

The aim of life coaching is centered around individual development and growth in various aspects of a person's life. The idea behind this practice is to help individuals come up with the best answers on their own. Life coaches approach their clients with the mindset that they have all of the answers inside of them. They just need guidance to get there. Life coaches help their clients through a variety of techniques, and the most common one is asking the right questions.

Through the coaching process, people can develop a work-life balance, improve their business, start valuing their relationships, take care of their health, and just live a more functional life. How can a life coach do this? By helping you clarify your goals, identify obstacles that are in the way, prioritize what's important, and come up with strategies to start making the proper adjustments. As we mentioned before, the client comes up with the solutions, which is the best part because they maintain control of their lives. The following are some of the indications for needing a life coach:

- Having constant stress and worry, sometimes, for no apparent reason at all
- Not having any direction in life; having no idea where to go or how to get there
- Having difficulty in making decisions, whether they are easy or difficult
- Persistently feeling dissatisfied with work, relationships, and anything else
- Not having any fulfillment in life, even while doing the things you enjoy

While there may be some overlap, life coaching is not the same as counseling, therapy, or consulting. These are different fields and you should not mix them up. Unlike coaching, practitioners in these fields are more likely to tell you what to do. Coaches will never tell you what to do, but simply guide you. In addition, life coaches do not deal with medical issues, like mental health disorders. The clients who seek out a life coach are not doing so for any illness, but to achieve more value in their lives.

In our second book, *Who Wants To Be a Superhero If You Can Be a Business Coach?*, we discussed business coaching, which is just one of the subsets of life coaching. These types of coaches help their clients with strategies and techniques to help improve their business and entrepreneurial endeavors. Once again, a business coach will not give you advice but help you come up with ways to grow and expand your business, leading to more clients and more annual revenue. A good coach is worth their weight in gold, especially since they will have an objective bird's-eye view of which direction needs to be taken.

This brings us to our third book that you are reading now, which covers leadership coaching. Leadership coaches work with high-level achievers and motivated individuals, like CEOs of major corporations, politicians, organizers, and ambitious entrepreneurs. When working with any of these individuals, they will help them achieve an even higher level of success, beyond anything they could have ever imagined before.

The impact from a leadership coach will feel like a ripple effect across an entire organization or group. As clients begin following the guidance of their coach, the skills they obtain will help everyone else around them, by bringing more clarity to the situation and direction for finding the correct solutions. Basically, as a person works with a leadership coach, they develop more qualities of a leader, which will be beneficial for everyone. A leader sets the tone for the environment they are in, so when they are happy, effective, strong, and focused, their entire team will be the same way.

While a leadership coach will help maximize their clients' performance in the business world, their advice and support will positively transform their personal lives. The world is becoming much more fast-paced and this phenomenon will not be slowing down any time soon. Instagram, Facebook, YouTube, TikTok, and other similar platforms are running wild. This means there are tremendous opportunities for immediate success and failure. With so much confusion and chaos going on, people are in need of guidance and clarity like never before. This is where the skills of a leadership coach come in. Through deep listening and careful questioning, a coach will help remove the obstacles standing in their leadership client's way so they can achieve their desired goals.

Just like any other type of life coach, a leadership coach will never solve their client's problems. They will simply help them clarify their goals, aid in finding solutions, and come up with the right action steps to move their goals forward. With each session, the coach will follow up on the progress that is made and hold their clients accountable.

Many leaders out there have the technical excellence, training, knowledge, and resources they need. The problem is that their judgment is clouded and they have no idea which direction to take. It is similar to having a reliable car that can get you to any destination, but not knowing exactly where you are, where you want to go, or how to get there. In this example, the problem is not the car, but where exactly you want to take it. The same holds true for the leader. In this scenario, they do not need more training, just more guidance. They need something much more personal and involved, like leadership coaching.

If you speak to many high-achieving individuals, no matter what industry they are in, they will probably have a coach, or several coaches, in their corner. In fact, the reason they are at their current level is that they have coaches. There's a good chance they hired a coach well before reaching their current level. Therefore, if you don't feel that you've accomplished what you have wanted to in life, it may be time to go the route of hiring a coach. If you want to start winning in life, no matter what your current status is, going the route of leadership coaching can help you out tremendously.

WHAT TO LOOK FOR IN A LEADERSHIP COACH

The relationship you have with a leadership coach needs to be something special, just like with any other form of life coaching. You will be investing a significant amount of time and money, so the benefit you receive needs to far outweigh the investment you make. You will already be busy enough running your business, moving up the career ladder, and managing things at home. The last thing you want to worry about is whether the relationship with your coach is positive or not.

Once you find the right coach in this field, you will see your success skyrocket, as long as you do your part, as well. We will go over some ways to maximize your return on investment and get the most out of every session you take part in.

Make Sure It's a Good Match

Your first objective is to find a coach you are comfortable with and can respect. While there needs to be a comfort level, the coach must also challenge you. This is the only way that growth will occur. When we speak of comfort here, we are referring more to trust, than feeling relaxed and laid-back. A good coach will support and encourage you every step of the way, but also provide tough love when necessary, especially when you are not doing your part. If you are not following through on what gets discussed during the sessions, then you are accountable for not making any progress. Any good leadership coach will make that clear to you.

A good coach will also have plenty of resources to provide for you. They will not give you any answers but will help you find the right ones that you need. Reputation matters greatly when it comes to coaching. Since coaching is not a regulated field, anyone can technically call themselves a leadership coach. This is why you must do your due diligence in researching candidates, including reviews from past clients. Even though a coach is not technically required to have certifications, you can still seek out the ones who do. Of course, training and certifications alone do not automatically convey talent. You must still look at their track record.

They Have a Vested Interest in You

A good coach sees their profession as more than a job. They see it as a calling. Therefore, they will always go above and beyond to make sure they can help you succeed. In many cases, this will mean working on their off hours, making follow-up phone calls, and making sure to keep track of your progress. A good coach will not just go through the motions. They will be heavily engaged with you and have a vested interest in your progress. Not just because you paid them, but because they genuinely want you to succeed in your business or organization.

They Never Stop Learning

Successful leadership coaches must have the same mindset as any other successful individual in that they never stop learning. If you have a coach who acts like they know it all, it might be time to show them the door. If they are not willing to grow, they cannot help you grow. Seek out leadership coaches who enjoy reading, studying, and speaking with other knowledgeable people. If your coach seems to be interested in learning from you, that is a good sign.

They Will Help You Set Goals

A leadership coach should help their clients set ambitious goals. By this, we don't just mean asking their clients what their goals are. As people, we often set the bar low for ourselves. Instead of reaching for bigger things, we play it safe and hope to just barely make it alive. A strong coach can inspire you to get out of your comfort zone and set bigger goals for yourself.

Beyond setting goals, a leadership coach can help you visualize and come up with proper action steps to achieve them. They will also encourage you every step of the way, whether times are good or bad. If you don't feel like your coach is pushing you to be better, it's time to find someone new.

They Provide a Confidential Space

We spoke in our earlier books about the importance of confidentiality. You must always feel assured that whatever you are discussing during a coaching session is not leaving the walls of that meeting. If you don't feel like you can trust your coach in this manner, that's a problem. It will ultimately hinder what you are willing to say. Being able to keep conversations private is a hallmark of good coaching practice.

Overall, these are the minimum qualities any leadership coach should bring to the table. This will help ensure you have a positive coaching experience.

Privacy

THE PERSONALITY OF A GOOD COACH

While almost anyone can train to be a good coach, there are certain personality traits that will give a person an edge in this industry. If you want to become a good coach, you can start to develop these qualities within yourself.

Have an Organized Approach/Commitment

Good coaches are organized, whether it comes to keeping track of paperwork or making sure the sessions stay on track. Being organized shows that the coach is committed to their craft because they are taking the time to make sure things are running smoothly. Therefore, a coach will make sure clients are scheduling their appointments as needed, keep records of what was discussed, and make sure that sessions do not go off the rails. An organized and committed approach shows clients that a coach cares about their success.

Imagine going into an appointment and the individual is completely scattered. They have no idea what is happening and seem like they forgot about the appointment, overall. Chances are, you would not want to go back to this person again.

Process-Oriented/Consistent

Coaching sessions are certainly customized to the client's needs, but there needs to be some consistency with each session. With such consistency, the client will not be left confused and wondering what they are supposed to do. A good coaching session has the following components:

- Standards: Have a certain set of rules
- Monitoring: Monitor progress
- Analysis: Analyze what is happening
- Feedback: Give your client constructive feedback

There should not be a "shoot from the hip" approach to a coaching session. It needs to be reliable and predictable, for the most part. Surprises should only be used sparingly for strategic purposes. You can make adjustments along the way, but for the most part, there needs to be a routine process.

Objectivity

Good coaches do not work based on biases. They are objective in their approach, whether talking to a client the first time or giving feedback. There should be no personal feelings involved. This will make the relationship more meaningful in that the information provided will be honest and open.

Balanced/Fair

People are more likely to give negative feedback than positive feedback. People's minds tend to swerve towards negativity. Good coaches are conscious of this and try to be balanced. People do not want to hear negative feedback all the time. Also, the feedback should not have positivity and negativity mixed into it. Instead, discuss the positive items and then the negative ones. Keep them both separated. This way, there is no mixing of messages, which will avoid confusion.

Tough/Firm

At some point, you will have to be tough and firm with your clients. especially when they are not doing what they said they would. This goes along with holding someone accountable. If you and a client come up with a goal and a deadline, it must be followed. Do not fall for excuses because everyone will have them.

Flexibility

A great coach should be able to adjust to each client based on which client they are working with. For example, some clients appreciate more direct communication, while others need to be handled more gently. There may be a feeling out process at the beginning, but eventually, the coach will learn who they are dealing with.

Realistic

Great coaches are optimistic about what they can do and will try to work with almost anybody. They will give their clients as many chances as they can. But to be effective, a good coach has to see the client and the coaching relationship realistically. Eventually, a coach will have to move on if there is no progress being made. This means they will have to cut ties with a client and advise them to go elsewhere to get coaching, if they choose to do so. These instances are rare but still occur. As a coach, you must recognize when your efforts become moot.

HOW TO GET THE MOST OUT OF A COACHING SESSION

After finding a good coach that fits your unique personal needs, you will need to hold up your end too. Remember that the coach is not there to solve your problems. That is not even remotely what they are there for. Instead, they will provide expert guidance through their unique methods and it is your job to follow through on actions. In this section, we will go over how you can get the most out of your coaching session, so you are not wasting anyone's time, especially your own.

Set Realistic Goals

You should expect to make regular progress as you continue to work with a leadership coach. However, be realistic and do not expect major changes to occur overnight. Communicate candidly with your coach about where you are and where you want to be. Once you establish this, you can set attainable goals. Break them down into daily, weekly, monthly, annually, and so on. Major change actually occurs from minor changes that build up over time.

Unfortunately, too many people only see the end result of success and not all of the work that led up to it. If you are not used to being a leader, it will take a while for you to become comfortable in this role, no matter what environment you are in.

Enjoy Learning

Just like you would expect your coach to be a voracious learner, you must be the same way. Always be curious, take notes, and determine ways in which you can educate yourself. Be self-aware of your knowledge and always come to every session willing and ready to learn. If you don't, you will just be wasting your time.

Learning

Be Unapologetically Honest

Hopefully, you have taken the time to find a coach that you trust. Once you have this established, you must be ready to be completely honest with yourself and your coach. If you are not upfront about the strengths and weaknesses of your leadership style, your coach will not be able to help you. When you are radically honest, you will begin to learn from your failures and missed opportunities, evolve your goals, and develop a growth mindset.

This honesty goes both ways. If you feel that your coach could do more to help you, don't be shy about letting them know. You are the one making an investment in the coaching session, so the approach they use needs to work for you. A good relationship with a coach will provide invaluable benefits to your success as a leader. However, the time your spend with them will be limited. Therefore, you need to make sure you are optimizing every session. Don't forget to show up with an open mind that is ready for feedback.

Push Yourself

Your coach will provide support, encouragement, and accountability. Beyond that, they will not be able to go inside your body and physically push you. You must be ready to do that yourself. The goal of having a coach is to become the best leader you can be. For this to occur, you must challenge yourself every day. Ask your coach for honest feedback and take what they say seriously.

It is hard to get feedback you don't like. However, that is the only way to know where you are struggling. Not everything can be wrapped up in a neat, pretty package. You will probably have your feelings hurt once in a while, but this will help you out greatly in the long run. Trust us, your coach does not mean to hurt your feelings, but they have to be honest in order to give you the most help.

Ask for Help

The reason you are working with a coach is that you need help to become a better leader. Take advantage of this support and don't be shy about asking for help. Also, don't be afraid to be vulnerable. Being vulnerable is actually a sign of courage because you are taking a risk by putting your emotions out there. Many people who seek out coaches are Type A personalities who believe that they are being weak when asking for help. However, this could not be farther from the truth. Turning to a coach for help actually makes you wise.

Whether you plan to work with a leadership coach or become one yourself, you will need to have certain attributes to succeed. As we go through this book, we will get more in-depth about specific coaching and leadership qualities. In chapter two, we will describe the importance of leadership coaching.

HOW CAN ORGANIZATIONS BENEFIT MOST FROM LEADERSHIP COACHES?

Not only will leadership coaches help individual leaders, but they will also provide benefits to organizations they are involved with as a whole. The success of coaching depends on the skills of the coach and team member's willingness to learn and grow. No matter how great a leadership coach is, if the client is not receptive, the sessions will not get very far. In this section, we will cover some effective ways to set up success for both the client and coach.

Provide Access

Many coaches are able to work with limited information, however, the more access they have, the greater the potential for positive results. This is because the coach will have a greater understanding of the organization, including its history, values, leadership models, and current challenges. Once they can gather more information, they will be able to provide better feedback for improvement. As much as possible, allow the coach to interact with team members and observe them in their natural environments. Greater access will help the coach and client in a number of ways:

- They will be able to get the full story from all team members so they can better understand and improve those relationships.

- They will be able to help business leaders build alliances with organizational partners.
- They can help clarify any miscommunication and provide specific advice.

Reinforce Credibility

If you bring in a coach to help your organization, we assume you believe in their talents and abilities. Your team members must feel the same way. While it's ultimately up to the coach to win the trust of an organization, you can do your part to build up their credibility. Make it clear through your words and actions that you are treating them like a true partner. Every time you introduce the coach to your team, do not just make a general announcement. Mention the specific abilities of the coach and how they will be able to improve things for everyone involved. From here, it is up to the coach to live up to his or her reputation.

Set Clear Expectations

Simply put, for a coaching-client relationship to work, clear expectations must be placed. These need to be discussed beforehand; otherwise, there will be a lot of contention along the way. Make sure to understand what the role of a coach is, compared to an advisor or consultant.

Avoid Power Struggles

There needs to be a close relationship between coaches and their clients, which is the organization as a whole in this case. Also, the coach needs to be given respect and credibility, as we mentioned before. That being said, the coach should not be overhyped and made out to be more than they are. A coach is there to ask questions, observe, and provide guidance. They are not there to take over anyone else's job.

SETTING UP A COACHING SESSION

When two or more people are having a conversation, things can easily go haywire and everyone will start going off on tangents. A conversation can start in one area and be about something completely different a few minutes later. This is okay if you're having a regular conversation with a friend, but if you plan on having a productive coaching session, there needs to be more organization. The following are some steps to help structure a coaching session:

- Establish a coaching agreement: Identify what is important about the session and what all parties plan to accomplish by the end.
- Set the goal: Ask the client what their desired outcome is for the session. How will you know when the goal has been achieved? What will it look and feel like?
- Start the actual coaching: Starting with the desired

outcome, invite the client to explore different actions for discovering possible solutions.

- Identify and commit to action: The client will choose what actions they will commit to. What might get in the way of accomplishing goals? How will the client support their commitment to action?

- Key outcomes: What are the main takeaways from the previous session? What new things were learned about? What new things are the coach and client aware of?

- Accountability: The coach gets together with the client to discuss the promises being kept for the next session. How will the client hold themselves accountable for the goals set today? How can the coach support their client to hold them accountable?

A version of these steps should be followed. The bottom line is that coaching sessions should not be a free-for-all. There needs to be some kind of blueprint to hold everything together. If not, both the client and the coach are wasting their time.

Organization

CREATING A LEADERSHIP COACHING CAREER

As coaches ourselves, we understand the value the profession brings to everyone involved. We learn just as much from our clients as they do from us. As you read through the following chapters, we are confident that you will want to become a leadership coach yourself one day, which we would be thrilled about. We need more coaches out there helping us, and what better way to know if you are a fit by getting help from your own coach.

People come to the coaching profession from different outlets. You do not need a background in counseling, teaching, healthcare, or anything else. Mainly, you need to have a passion for the industry. Of course, for leadership coaching, a background in business is definitely helpful. There is a need out there for leaders, and leadership coaches are the perfect people to help create these individuals. You will definitely keep yourself busy. We will go over some things to help you become successful in the field.

New Career!

Have a Sound Coaching Philosophy

A sound coaching philosophy is a foundation you will work from when dealing with clients. You will be coaching a diverse group of people with a variety of life experiences, from management to CEOs, to business owners, and various other group leaders. Also, you may be coaching individuals or small groups. While each client will have different needs, having a coaching philosophy will determine how you approach a session. The clients you work with expect highly customized and confidential counsel. With a coaching philosophy, you will be able to go into each session with more confidence.

There are three factors that a sound coaching philosophy should include:

- Describe the purpose of leadership coaching and help others appreciate the vision and mission of the coach.
- The philosophy should align with the core values and beliefs of the coach.
- It should help prospective clients understand the value they can expect to experience by working with a leadership coach.

The coaching process is guided by mutual trust between the coach and client. During the partnership, the leader will receive customized feedback and guidance to maximize personal, professional, and organizational performance. Be ready to articulate your coaching philosophy with any client right from the beginning.

Understand the Difference Between Coaching and Advising

We covered this a lot in our previous books, but just as a reminder, coaching is not the same as advising. It is important to know this before going in. While there is some crossover, they are separate fields. They both add institutional value for delivering results, but they take a different approach. The objective of a leadership coach is to assist clients in making behavioral changes that will lead to positive results. An advisor, on the other hand, takes a results-oriented approach, and if there's time, they might work on behavior and develop skills, but there is no guarantee.

As a coach, you are teaching your clients how to fish, rather than giving them a fish. Therefore, you have the potential to create a long-lasting impact. Your job when working with leaders is to channel their inner strength and pull the best out of them. After working with you, they will realize the potential that they have and this is the true beauty of being a coach.

Design a Coaching Methodology and Process

If you decide to enter the realm of leadership coaching, you must determine to what extent this will occur. Do you plan on adding it as a component to an existing career, like being a manager or supervisor, or do you intend to create a whole new career out of it? Of course, you can always decide to switch things up later, but it's definitely good to have an idea of which direction you want to go. If you want to make a career change, then a significant commitment will be needed.

A proper leadership coaching methodology and process will provide for many factors that will work to serve your clients the best. These factors include:

- A process for assessing the chemistry between a coach and client—No matter how great of a coach you are, you will not be a match for everybody. Do not take this personally because there are many factors at play. Your coaching process should consider how you will figure out the best coach/client match.
- How will you address issues of confidentiality, define specific roles, set expectations, and create metrics that evaluate performance outcomes?
- How will you align your coaching philosophy with the coaching framework?
- A process for ensuring both the coach and client will be held accountable—Yes, the coach is responsible to their clients, as well.
- A strategy to evaluate the kind of issues, challenges, and problems you will agree to solve or improve
- Methods to describe the purpose, competencies, and behaviors required for positive results

Establish a Consistent Pricing Model

When you get right down to it, leadership coaching is a business. Therefore, one of your goals is to create income, and your clients will want to know how much they will be paying. These are legitimate concerns because people work hard for their money. They want to make sure it is spent wisely. Whether you do coaching as a side gig or build a successful career from it, you will have to develop a pricing model and determine what your fees will be.

You can mimic some of these pricing models:

- Lump-sum payment or package pricing model
- Daily or weekly pricing model
- Membership pricing model
- Performance-based pricing model (pay based on results)
- Hourly-rate pricing model

Your clients should not be shocked or blindsided by your prices. You need to be transparent with them from the beginning because that is just good business practice. Your pricing needs to be competitive but should not undercut your talents. Do not be afraid to charge what you think you're worth because you are running a business, after all. There are a few criteria to consider when setting up your fees:

- How long have you been coaching and what are your credentials? While coaching is not a regulated field and there are technically no educational requirements, having certifications and licenses can make you more marketable.
- How do you deliver your coaching methods (in-person, video conferencing, webcam, phone, or email, etc.)?
- Are you working with individual contracts or organizations?
- How many clients do you have and what is your overall experience?

We hope this information serves you well on your coaching journey. There is still plenty more information to go.

Pricing

2

THE IMPORTANCE OF LEADERSHIP COACHING

Picture yourself driving on the road headed to a destination. You know where you want to go, but don't really know how to get there. To help you in this situation, you decide to ask for directions, buy maps, and use a GPS. These tools are used to help you get where you want to be. You will also see some interesting things along the way. Think of a leadership coach in the same way. They are someone who can guide you in finding the right paths to get to a destination or life goal.

After reading our first two books, you probably have a good idea of the benefits of life coaching. Here, we will get much more in-depth about the importance of leadership coaching and the advantages it can bring for you in life. After establishing the effectiveness of this coaching practice, we will get into more detail about leadership, specifically, in the next chapter. Get ready to enjoy the ride.

WHAT MAKES LEADERSHIP COACHING IMPORTANT?

If you look at different organizations, you will witness a variety of practices being performed based on company culture and values. However, while methods will be different, one of the main constants will be the importance of good leadership. No matter what industry or customer base an organization is geared towards, it will not function appropriately without the presence of strong leaders who serve as the backbone of the organization.

Those who have never experienced good leadership do not realize how beneficial it can be. On the other hand, those who are in the presence of good leadership don't realize what they have until it's gone. Even though leaders serve as the core of any unit, group, or organization, leadership development statistics have produced shocking results in showing that 71% of companies feel that their current group of leaders are not ideal for their future plans. This is definitely alarming because if there is poor leadership at the top, a business will suffer throughout its entire existence.

To combat these negative statistics, many organizations are already turning to leadership coaches in the hopes of developing more effective leaders in the long run. Leadership skills can always be taught. While it may sound strange to coach leaders, it can truly improve work quality when done the right way.

This means that both the coach and client must do their part. In a major study done of Fortune 1000 companies, 48% of their leaders who experienced coaching showcased higher performance levels. This led to higher productivity and engagement. As a result, companies continue to seek out leadership coaches, and the demand will continue to grow.

Once you begin working with a leadership coach, you will start understanding what positive changes can come from the practice. If you decide to become a leadership coach in the future, you will be able to inspire others to start leading their team well, in whatever environment they are in. We will go over some key advantages that leadership coaching can produce.

Empowerment

The coaching practice can empower leaders to do work that is extraordinary. A coach can provide an objective outlook that proves advantageous to the client. They will be able to uncover the hidden strengths and weaknesses of a leader. Through coaching sessions and follow-up communications, a coach and client will develop a strong bond, which will allow them to create goals to help pinpoint weaknesses and track progress.

With the hustle and bustle of everyday life, individuals often neglect the person who needs the most improvements, and that is themselves. By working with a coach, a leader is able to reflect on their life, current situation, past mistakes and accomplishments, and plans for the future. These reflective sessions will allow an individual to understand their present status, the improvements they have made, and the work they have done to meet their personal goals.

New Insights

As a leader, it is easy to become overwhelmed with all of the responsibility thrown your way. While it is nice to have people look up to you, it can also be stressful. As a result, it can be difficult to solve the immense number of problems that have to be dealt with. When a coach is there to help, a leader can gain new insight into everyday responsibilities. They can help the leader take a step back and reflect on why things are not going as they should. There may be some deeper problems that need to be confronted. From here, the coach and client can create a new plan to overcome similar situations in the future because of the new perspective that is gained.

Free Thinking

Leadership coaches can encourage their clients to stop thinking in a narrow-minded way. Instead, leaders will begin opening up their thought patterns and consider different points of view that would have never crossed their minds before. This will benefit leaders by allowing them to think more freely and lead with more flexibility. Free thinking allows for quicker, more creative, and more precise decision-making skills in different situations, especially those under pressure.

Enhanced Performance

Even the best leaders have weaknesses. A leadership coach can target their practice towards a leader's problem areas. This can make a huge difference in their attitude and performance. The many new techniques that a leader can learn will help them reach individuals on their team who were not responsive to their approach before. Overall, the leader will become more effective. We will get into more detail about leadership techniques in Chapter Four.

Improved Communication

Leaders need to have clear and effective communication skills. Unfortunately, many do not and don't even realize it. As a result, their team members become more confused and misdirected. Coaching enables leaders to recognize their faulty communication skills and discover what specific weaknesses they have.

Leadership coaches can also teach clients how to communicate properly with people of different cultures, backgrounds, personality types, and ages. A leader will have to deal with all sorts of people, and the most successful ones can build a good rapport with almost anybody. This does not mean you have to like all people. It simply means you have to build some type of working relationship together.

The world is a diverse place, but with good communication skills, people from all over the world can connect to each other.

Remember that communication is not just verbal. Things like body language, eye contact, and tone of voice are also important components. A good leadership coach can guide leaders to communicate more effectively in every aspect and improve their credibility and skills.

WHAT DOES LEADERSHIP COACHING ENTAIL?

Since you will have a lot of responsibility as a leader, it is important for you to perform at your full potential. If not, you are cheating yourself and your team members. A coach will use a variety of methods to enhance your leadership capabilities. The specifics of their approach will depend on numerous factors, including style, personality traits, and strengths. Coaches are people, and therefore they also have unique practices that they prefer. Just like any other type of life coach, a leadership coach will not give you orders to follow but guide you to finding the right answers within yourself. The following are some common methods that many coaches use:

- Taking the time to gather and analyze important data regarding the behavioral qualities of a leader and an organization—This includes the performance of the managers and team members. This data can be used to determine team dynamics within a group.
- Meeting with leaders on a regular basis to discuss

specific issues and plans to proceed for the future—
Working with a coach is rarely a "one and done" deal.
You will need frequent sessions to get the full benefit
from them. In fact, once you begin working with a
good coach, it will be difficult to stop.

- Addressing a wide array of concerns, as well as offering
  personal support and guidance

- Providing many resources and tools, like educational
  courses, reading material, technology, and various
  types of educational opportunities

- Assisting with setting and following-through on goals
  by holding their clients accountable for what they say
  and do—It's easy to talk about doing something and
  then forget about it down the line. This won't be the
  case with a good coach. They will not let you get away
  with meaningless talk without real action.

- Offering professional feedback on a leader's individual
  skills and progress

BENEFITS OF LEADERSHIP COACHING

When you watch children play together, you may notice them
taking on various roles. Some will automatically take charge,
run the show, and tell the other kids what to do. Others will
simply go along to get along. The point here is that some people
are born with leadership skills and showcase them at a very
early age. Some people develop these skills because of their

education and surroundings. Of course, anyone can still learn to be leaders later on in their lives, even if they never had any of these attributes before.

No matter where you fall on the spectrum, you can create and hone your leadership skills using a variety of techniques. Purposefully putting yourself in situations of leadership can also force you to become a more effective leader. Of course, working with a leadership coach is one of the most efficient ways to build up all of your skills. There are a large number of benefits that come from this coaching field, which we will discuss in greater detail here.

Gaining a New Perspective

After spending so much time inside your company's unique culture, it is natural to get trapped in their day-to-day business and lose sight of the bigger picture. Soon enough, we can all end up working day and night but don't understand where we are headed. A leadership coach can help you gain a new perspective in this regard. A leadership coach has likely worked with many different organizations and leaders, so they are aware of many dynamics. This means the coach has a lot of insight into what actually works and what doesn't; therefore, you can spend less time on methods that are pointless and more time on those that are effective. In addition, a coach can help you come up with new ways to solve problems, no matter how big or small, and how to bring out the talents of your employees.

Higher Company Performance Within the Industry

The direction of a company depends on having strong leadership. Therefore, leaders are essential for the success of any company. As you attend each coaching session, it will become apparent that you are not the only one who is benefiting from them. Your organization as a whole and the people who work for it will also grow tremendously. This is because you will develop new strategies and set up new goals that will help your entire company.

There will be a lot of companies within your industry, which means you will have much competition to contend with. When your employees are happier and more productive, you will have a competitive edge and see better results in all aspects of your business. This will eventually lead to higher profit margins.

You'll Gain Confidence and Self-Awareness

Being a leader is hard and when you are new to this type of role, it can be very overwhelming and stressful. It is easy to lose faith in your abilities and believe you are not good enough to lead others. On top of that, learning and education are endless pursuits. No matter what role you are in, you can never stop learning and growing. Otherwise, you will be left behind and never achieve the success you were meant for.

Seeking out new ways to tackle your work is important because your job will always be changing with various advancements. A good relationship with your coach will help you discover your hidden strengths and talents. Recognizing these unknown skills can help build your confidence and self-awareness, making you grow as a leader.

You'll Become a Better Leader

This one is obvious and the whole point of hiring a leadership coach. If you are not receiving this benefit, then it is pointless to hire a coach. Your coach will use different methods based on what they know and are comfortable with. However, no matter what approach they use, their objective must be to help you: improve, make better decisions, become more self-aware about your choices and why you make them, improve your ability to delegate and recognize the competencies of those around you, and develop steps you can take to advance your career and improve the outlook of your company. Overall, you will become better at your job with the help of a leadership coach.

Being a leader is an important job because the decisions you make will not only impact you—they might even affect millions of people around the world. Think about individuals like the owners of worldwide corporations, captains of sports teams, or even the President of the United States. Imagine how many people are affected by the direction these people decide to go in. Guess what? They all surround themselves with people, like coaches, advisors, or consultants, who are highly knowledgeable in their field and can help them make the best decisions possible. Why should you not do the same thing with a leadership coach? This is an important tool that you should never overlook.

The objective here is not about overhauling your leadership style—of course, unless you choose to go down this path. The ultimate goal is actually to identify strengths and weaknesses so that you can develop your leadership skills and learn more effective strategies for bettering yourself and your organization.

We are just getting started in discussing the benefits of leadership coaching. If you are interested in going down this route, keep reading about the personal and professional advantages you will gain.

SUCCESSFUL PEOPLE WHO USED LEADERSHIP COACHES

If all of the information we have gone over has not convinced you of the benefits of leadership coaching, then perhaps you would like to know about how real people have benefited from leadership coaching. There are plenty of successful people in the business and entrepreneurial world who have used business coaches in their own lives. They believed in the power of coaching and their results speak for them.

Coaches are not just for beginners. In many cases, the individual is a master at their craft. The coach is just able to help them hone their skills, become more focused, and become even better.

Let's use the example of a sports team. All teams have coaches, but they do not have more skills than the players. However, they have knowledge, insight, and the ability to motivate their players to perform at a higher level. The same concept holds true for leadership coaching. We will go over some leaders in the business world who used coaches to improve their outcomes (webadmin, 2019).

Bill Gates

Bill Gates is the well-known co-founder and co-creator of Microsoft. He has served many roles within the corporation, including CEO and chief software architect. He is a man of many talents. Even while having some powerful positions in his company, Gates has used leadership coaches before. During a Ted Talk in 2013, he stated that everyone should have a coach, no matter what trade or at what level. It is not just for high-level executives or people who are struggling. Individuals from all backgrounds can learn from the coaching process.

"Everyone needs a coach. We all need people who will give us feedback. That's how we improve."

— BILL GATES

Steve Jobs

Steve Jobs is another household name after he rose to fame as the co-founder of Apple, serving as both the chairman and CEO. Jobs had worked with different coaches throughout the years and according to statements by them, he was very interested in learning about himself from an outside perspective. Through his coaching experience, Jobs increased his self-awareness and learned to listen better to those around him.

According to one of his coaches, John Mattone, Steve Jobs was curious to discover more about himself, how other people perceived him, and how he could be a more effective leader. In many ways, he was different from the caricature of the difficult manager that many people had heard about (webadmin, 2019).

Eric Schmidt

Eric Schmidt is the former CEO of Google and Executive Chairman of Alphabet, which is a parent company of Google. Schmidt was not keen on hiring a leadership coach when he first heard about it. He did not think he needed help because of the success he had already experienced. He finally acquiesced and decided to try it out. After doing so, he admitted that it was the best advice anyone had ever given him. He quickly learned that people are not good at determining how others see them. A coach can really help in this regard (webadmin, 2019).

We are sure you recognized at least some of these names. The reason these individuals reached the level that they did was because they were not afraid to admit they needed to improve. Asking for help shows that you have strength and is not a sign of weakness. Also, those who refuse to learn are doomed to mediocrity and that is not our motto at Elvin Coaches.

Success!

WHY DO HIGH PERFORMERS USE COACHES?

Think about some of the most talented actors in the world. They make great movies and make you either love or hate the character they are playing. What you may not know is that these talented individuals have many coaches who are helping them out behind the scenes. Why would these individuals need coaches if they already have the skills necessary? Because a coach can help hone these skills and guide these actors into becoming the best they can be.

A common misconception out there is that only people who are lost, confused, lazy, incompetent, or unmotivated need coaches. The truth is, everyone needs a coach and the ones who use them the most are high performers who are already towards the top of their industry. In fact, these individuals need coaches more than anyone else because leadership often does not come easy to them. We will go over a few reasons why.

Very Few People Are at the Level of High Performers

When you are a high performer, it is easy to stand out from the crowd because very few people are willing to do what you do. In the world we live in, only a small percentage of people put in the work, time, effort, dedication, and sacrifice to reach the top level in any industry. We are not saying most people are lazy. They just don't have the same drive as the one or two percent of the population who consistently achieve great results.

It can also be frustrating to perform at high levels because it is harder to relate to people. These individuals either ignore those who are not at their level because they feel they are beneath them, or they try to tear them down. Working with a leadership coach can help them deal with the frustration of not fitting in and see it as more of a blessing. Once this mindset develops, the high performers can start lifting others up.

They Are Hard on Themselves and Others

High performers have extremely high expectations for themselves. This causes them to push themselves harder than anyone else ever could so they continue to perform better. This can create many emotional and physical problems, as they are way too busy trying to succeed and don't take the time to care for their needs. Another downside is that these high performers will push their expectations onto other people. At some point, these expectations become unattainable. People can start to find this deflating. The bar does not have to be lowered, but there are ways to have a high bar without driving everyone crazy. A good coach can guide a high achiever in not taking things so seriously and helping them understand how other people view them.

They Are Great at What They Do, But Can't Break It Down for Other People

At some point, high performers become so good at their craft that they can do it in their sleep. This is great for them but not anybody else. The reason is they cannot describe the process of what they do so it can be replicated by others. When things come naturally to them, they have a hard time imagining why other people cannot perform the tasks just as well. A leadership coach can help these individuals take a step back and start defining what they do as a process. This will help them become more relatable and even valuable to their team members.

It's Hard for Them To Understand That Others Are Different

Some performers get so caught up in how they do things that they cannot fathom other people doing things differently. The truth is that people get results in different ways. There is more than one way to skin a cat, as the old expression goes. With the right coaching, high performers can start dealing with the differences in others, which will improve their cohesiveness with teammates.

High performers are generally the ones who end up leading people because they have the attribute to influence change. Unfortunately, leadership does not always come naturally to them because of the reasons described above. However, after working with a leadership coach, these high performers can become exceptional leaders. When a high performer gains necessary leadership skills, the magic starts to happen.

THE GREAT COMMUNICATORS

Whether you are a coach, leader, or both, you will need excellent communication skills to be effective. Many people think they are good communicators, but if they were to be on the other end and listen to themselves speak, they might have a different opinion. Whatever the case, you need to improve your skills as a communicator so people will understand you. You will be more influential in this manner because great communicators inspire people. We will go over some strategies that can significantly help you in this regard.

Speak to Groups as Individuals

On numerous occasions you will have to speak to a group of people. You will not always have the luxury of speaking to someone one-on-one. You need to approach each person with a level of intimacy that makes them feel as though you are speaking directly to them. The trick is to eliminate the distraction of having a crowd. Deliver your message as if you are talking to a single person. You want to exude the same energy and attention as you would during a one-to-one session.

Talk in a Way So That People Will Listen

Simply being able to talk does not make you a great communicator. Anyone can babble on incessantly and make no sense whatsoever. Great communicators can read their audience, whether it is a group or one person, carefully, so they will not waste their breath reciting words that have no impact. You must speak in a way that gets people's attention and has them listening. This means that you might need to adjust your message on the fly. In the process of coaching, this can mean asking the right questions. If you get responses, you are on the right track.

Listen So People Will Talk

Communication is not just about the words you use. It also means how well you listen. Many leaders and coaches will treat communication as a one-way street. This is a disastrous approach for any coaching session. As a good communicator, you need to give people ample time to get their point across. If you find yourself always getting in the last word, it is a bad sign.

When someone is speaking to you, stop everything else and listen to what they have to say. Listen to their tone, volume, voice speed, and any hidden messages. Is there anything that is not being said or topics being avoided? For example, if you are talking on the phone, do not type an email. When you are meeting in person, don't look at your cell phone. Listen intently to the person. These simple behaviors will help you stay in the present moment.

Connect Emotionally

People will often forget exactly what you told them, but they will never forget how you made them feel. If people do not connect with you on an emotional level, your words will have very little value for them. Many leaders feel they need to showcase a certain persona, which is not true. To connect with people emotionally, you need to be transparent. This will show that you are human. Open up about yourself and show them what drives you, what you care about, and what makes you get out of bed every day.

Read Body Language

Leaders and coaches can come with a little authority, which makes it difficult for people to open up to you before you gain their trust. Read body language to determine what their words are not saying. This is where the greatest wealth of information lies. Therefore, watch body language any time you are communicating with someone, whether in a group or one-to-one session.

Practice Active Listening

Active listening is a great technique to ensure that people feel heard. To practice this strategy:

- Spend more of your time listening than speaking. This is basic math. The less time you spend doing one thing, the more you can spend on something else.
- Do not finish other people's sentences for them.
- Focus more on the other person than on yourself.
- Reframe what the person said and put it back on them to make sure you heard everything correctly.
- Do not interrupt.
- Take notes if you need to. (Definitely do this for coaching sessions and team meetings.)
- Ask plenty of questions.

Skip the Jargon

Avoid using words and phrases that are exclusive to an industry. If people understand the jargon, it is harmless. But to those who are not privy to it, it can be very off-putting. Don't use business-speak unless you have to, and try to connect with people on a personal level.

Work on these different strategies for better communication on a regular basis. You can even use them in your everyday conversations. It may take time to become good at all of these, so don't take on too many of them at one time.

3

UNDERSTANDING LEADERSHIP

Up to this point, we have mainly been discussing what leadership coaching is. Of course, that is the main reason we wrote this book. However, in order to become an effective coach, you must also understand what leadership is and the essential qualities that all leaders must have no matter what strategies they decide to employ. Therefore, the focus of this chapter will be to detail the ins and outs of being a great leader. After reading this chapter, you will truly understand the respect level that comes with the role.

The interesting thing here is that leaders are actually coaches themselves. They have the ability to guide their team members and bring out their best qualities. Leaders are not necessarily assigned their roles. Most of them rise above the pack because of their skills, actions, and results. In fact, many individuals who find themselves in assigned leadership roles, like being a manager or supervisor, end up fizzling out because they don't possess the natural qualities of leadership. In many cases, someone who is not in the role at all ends up in the position because of how their team members gravitate towards them.

As you scan the chapter, you will begin understanding what a leader is. From here, you can begin the steps to become one in your own personal and professional life. You will quickly learn that the role is never handed to anyone on a silver platter. It must be earned through action. Let's get started on our journey.

WHAT IS LEADERSHIP?

Leadership is defined as a way to maximize the efforts of others towards the achievement of a common goal using the process of social influence. This definition is simple enough, yet many people do not fully understand what leadership entails—even those who have been in the role for years.

There have been many books written and seminars are given about what leadership is. The problem here is that there seems to be no congruence in thought about this role. Our goal in this section is to finally define the idea of being a great leader as clearly as we can. Before we get there, though, let's go over what leadership is not:

- It has nothing to do with superiority or hierarchy within a company. So, just because someone has been in a place longer does not mean they will be a better leader for a company. Leadership also does not kick in just because you reach a certain pay scale.

- Titles do not equate to leadership. We spoke about this earlier, but just because an individual has been given a title that denotes leadership does not mean they automatically become one. You don't need a title to lead and you can become a leader in any group you are involved in, whether personal or professional.

- Personality does not equate to leadership. People often assume that leaders have to be bombastic, domineering, and charismatic. While many leaders do display these attributes, they do not automatically translate to good leadership skills.

- Leading is not the same thing as managing. Generally, managers manage things, like schedules and events, and also plan, coordinate, monitor, and solve. Leaders actually lead people.

"Leadership is influence—nothing more, nothing less."

— JOHN MAXWELL

Now that we have established what leadership is not, we will now revisit what it actually is:

- Leadership does not come from authority or power, but rather, influence. Anyone can boss someone around. That does not mean they have good leadership skills.
- Leadership requires other people and implies they don't need to be reported to directly. They can glean from a leader simply by their presence.
- There are many styles and paths to good leadership and it is not exclusive to any distinct personality traits, attributes, or titles.
- Leadership does not exist if there is no intended outcome. Leaders lead for a purpose. They are not just wandering aimlessly with their team members. There needs to be a common goal.

One of the things that people neglect about leadership is the idea of maximizing effort. A leader should not simply influence people to work, but actually motivate them to perform at their highest level.

UNDERSTANDING LEADERSHIP

A good leader is capable of understanding people's motivations and encourages the participation of employees in a way that unites their personal needs and interests with the group's specific purpose. Leaders are not always the most popular people in groups. However, they are the best at unifying people together towards a common purpose. A leader has the ability to marshal those who collaborate with him to achieve particular end results.

In a certain way, leaders attach the self-interest of their workers to the general interests of the employer. Humans are complex beings with varying levels of emotions and they all have different responses to love, prestige, independence, and achievements. A leader will recognize how to manage these different traits in the people around them.

Entities like the military are the most recognizable in terms of understanding leadership. Therefore, people's minds automatically revert to the general or commander who rules with an iron fist. While this is a form of leadership, it is not the only kind that exists. In many cases, the strategies that are used by the military will not cross the spectrum and be successful in the civilian world. In defense of the military, a few critical considerations need to be made:

- Soldiers are headed onto a battlefield with the potential for death. In some cases, it is certain death. Men often have to be replaced without a second thought if they get killed because the battle will still continue. This is why they are often treated uniformly and mechanically without giving much thought to their individual needs.
- There needs to be a strong clarity about duties and

responsibilities, which is maximized by the autocratic chain of command.

Forcing individuals through threats or the possibility of rewards may work in the short term. However, for long-term success, team members must want to perform their tasks, whatever they might be. This is where the skills of a great leader come into play. Each player must want to carry out their part and the largest problem a leader has is finding ways to get people to cooperate.

Relating With People

There are two fundamental lessons a leader must learn before they can be successful: humans are complex and they are different. Human beings respond to different things in different ways, making it difficult to take a one-size-fits-all approach when trying to lead groups of people. Not only do people react to the dangling carrot as a reward, but also to things like ambition, patriotism, spiritual beliefs, doing good for the world, boredom, excitement, and many other thought patterns that make up who they are. Also, these various interests have different amounts of influence over each person. For example:

- A person may have a deep religious faith, but this quality is irrelevant in this place of work.
- Another individual may get strong satisfaction in solving intellectual problems and never finds out how

his interests in playing chess or figuring out
mathematical puzzles can be applied to his work.

- Finally, one person may lack meaningful relationships
at home and thirst for them at work, only to become
frustrated by their superior's inability to recognize or
take advantage of those needs.

The more adept a leader is at responding to individual patterns
of behavior, the better they will be at generating intrinsic
interest in the work they are tasked with doing. An ideal organization should have employees at every level that are able to
report to someone who is able to know their team members as
real people and not just numbers or statistics. In this way,
workers feel as though they are respected and valued.

A great leader must recognize the goals and purposes of those
they are leading and must be in a position to satisfy them. They
must also understand the implications of their own actions and
how they will either positively or negatively affect other people.
A leader realizes that he or she does not live in an isolated world
and that their thoughts and actions will ultimately impact those
around them. Finally, a leader must be consistent and clear in
his decisions.

Relationships

Understanding a Subordinate

There is a dynamic that exists between an employer and employee which can create psychological difficulties for a subordinate. A successful leader will recognize these difficulties because they know that many workers have been brought up to view their employers as their enemies. This is an unfortunate mindset to have because coworkers in any organization should see each other as partners, not rivals. Subordinates often have to take orders from their superiors, which limits their independent decision-making and judgment.

An effective leader has the capability of giving their team members a certain amount of independence without allowing them to go completely roughshod over everything. For instance, they can allow subordinates to develop programs and make realistic decisions that are within their skillset. However, a leader will also understand when a team member is well over their head and cannot make the appropriate choices for the situation they are in. Therefore, a clear line must be drawn between decisions that must be made by a leader and those that can be handled by a subordinate. Once these lines are drawn, they must not be transgressed without careful consideration. Basically, a leader will know when it's appropriate to delegate and what their team members can handle. They must also be receptive and understanding when their subordinates are honest with them about their limitations.

In an ideal situation, a subordinate should be free to operate within a certain capacity where they know they are supported, but do not feel like someone is looking over their shoulders. A leader or superior can make suggestions and clarify goals when needed, but the subordinate should still feel free to make necessary decisions.

8 ESSENTIAL QUALITIES FOR GREAT LEADERSHIP

There is a crisis around the world that many leaders are dealing with. Many workers do not trust the management of the organizations they work for. Employers also have to cater to the additional needs of newer generations, who have different views about many issues related to the workplace. These newer employees also do not feel empowered at work and will change careers often.

Many people in leadership roles are failing to hone a sense of trust and loyalty from their teammates. Fortunately, this can be fixed through a little education. Managers who display good leadership qualities can motivate their teams to accomplish great things. We have determined eight of the most essential qualities a leader must possess and will discuss those in this section.

Sincere Enthusiasm

You cannot fake enthusiasm for a business, its products, or its mission. It must be genuine or people will eventually figure it out. Employees can figure out insincere cheerleading if they have worked there long enough, especially if the leaders cannot walk their own talk. You may have noticed this with your own management at work. They will have staff meetings where they try to motivate people and act like they are by your side, but are never seen again outside of the meetings. Once in a while, they may come around and pretend like they are engaged, but it is obviously a farce.

This is not real leadership or enthusiasm. When leaders in any capacity show real enthusiasm for what they are doing, it is contagious. All of the team members will feel the excitement and become motivated to do the necessary work. A great example of this is Elon Musk. A teammate who worked with Musk during the early stages of SpaceX stated that his enthusiasm for space travel was the driving force behind the success of the project. It is what gave him the motivation to keep going and his staff to keep believing in the venture. As a leader, if you are not showing true enthusiasm for your work, you will be exposed eventually.

Integrity

Many leaders will hide things from their team members either because they are afraid of looking foolish, getting exposed, or ruining their chance for success, just to name a few things. However, this goes against the idea of integrity, which means you must do the right thing, no matter how difficult it is. Whether you are giving someone credit for the work they did, acknowledging your own mistakes, or putting safety and quality first, great leaders live with integrity every day. In order to show true integrity, you must do what's right, even if it's not the best thing for the current project or bottom line. It will be better for you down the line because people will have more trust and faith in you.

People can sniff out those who are being untruthful. This quality is very off-putting and will harm you tremendously in the long run. Individuals do not want to be led astray, and when they are, even your most loyal team members will leave you. When trust is lost, your reputation is gone and it is very difficult to get back.

Integrity

Great Communication Skills

Many of the tasks that leaders must perform, like motivating their team members, giving instructions, or handing out discipline, cannot be accomplished without proper communication. You cannot simply yell at people to get them to do things, nor can you be excessively nice and expect others to listen. It takes a lot more to become a skilled communicator and if you are not one, it will lead to poor results. Leaders who are not great communicators are considered weak and ineffective. No matter how many great ideas they have, if they cannot be expressed clearly, they will be useless. An important fact to remember is that communication is not only about speaking, but also listening. When you listen, it must be with the intent to learn something, and not so you can respond.

Loyalty

Leaders should definitely expect a certain amount of loyalty from their teammates, but also remember that it is reciprocal. They must express loyalty in tangible ways that will benefit their whole team. This is done by ensuring that everyone has the proper resources and training to do their jobs properly. A leader must also be an advocate and stand up for their team during times of crisis. Whether things are going good or bad, a leader stays by their teammates' side.

Leaders must see themselves as being in service to their team. This does not mean the group members own the leader, but that the leader does his or her best to ensure everyone around them is taken care of. When employees experience loyalty from leadership, they are more likely to give it back.

Decisiveness

Leaders do not simply make decisions because their position calls for it. This means that when they do decide on something, they stand behind it and take responsibility. Many leaders out there will take action and then blame it on the circumstances. For example, a common statement could be, "I am only doing this because the company is making me, so I am not responsible for how it turns out." With decision-making, they are willing to be accountable by taking a risk and knowing it may not work out. If they don't, a leader will take the blame and figure something out.

Leaders who are not decisive are often ineffective. While you can certainly take advice and guidance from people, working too hard on getting a consensus is a waste of time and will have many negative effects. Many leaders out there will try to keep the peace with everyone and make decisions that ultimately satisfy no one. You must understand that people will always disagree with your decisions, and you cannot allow this to stifle your decisiveness.

Managerial Competence

People often associate being able to do a job well with having good leadership skills. The truth is, there are many great workers who do not have the capability of being leaders because they lack certain necessary qualities. A leader must understand the company's products and services, along with the goals, processes, and procedures. Simply being good at one's job does not guarantee that these qualities exist. The sports world provides a great example of this. Many great players tried to become coaches after their days on the field were up. Unfortunately, many also could not make the transition because their skills on the field did not translate to the leadership skills needed to be a coach. A true leader must be able to mentor, inspire, motivate, and direct.

Empowerment

A good leader has the confidence and ability to train and develop those who are under them. This means that their followers will eventually become autonomous by gaining the necessary skills that are needed. Basically, the goal of a leader is to make sure their team members do not need them forever.

Once they are able to act independently of them, the leader has done their job.

Employee empowerment leads to better decision-making that will benefit the company and customers. Occasionally, this will mean allowing the employees to go off-script and not always follow the guided path.

Empowerment

Charisma

We mentioned earlier that the most charismatic person is not automatically the leader in a group. That being said, it is still a viable quality to have because people are more likely to follow those they like. People love charismatic individuals. The best leaders are definitely well-spoken, friendly, and approachable. They don't have to be the most entertaining people, but they must be able to excite others in their group. A charismatic person is someone who is relatable.

All of these above qualities are essential when talking about good leaders. Without any of them, a leader will fall short of their true potential. Because of this, their team members will not be able to perform at their peak levels and the organization, as a whole, will suffer.

4

HOW TO BUILD A TEAM AROUND YOU

"Individual commitment to a group effort—that is what makes a team work, a company work, a society work, a civilization work."

— VINCE LOMBARDI

L et's be realistic. No matter how independent you want to be, there is only so much you, or anyone else can do by themselves. However, with a team, people can move mountains. All of the stories you hear about people making it big by pulling themselves up their own bootstraps is completely false when you dig deep enough. Nobody makes it completely on their own, despite what they might say. People received help along the way and this does not make their accomplishments any less valuable.

The focus of this chapter will be the process of building a team, which is one of the primary purposes of being a leader. A great leader realizes they need a strong team to back them up, so they devote their practice to making this happen. Once a team is built, they must also be coached. True leadership is about working together in a team to reach a common goal. Members of a group do not have to like each other, but they must have a working relationship. If you work at a job, there are probably certain employees you don't click with. However, you still need to work together to get the job done, whatever it may be.

Leaders who are team-aware know when something has gone wrong and take responsibility for it. On the other hand, when things go well, they reward the group for winning as a team.

THE UBUNTU PHILOSOPHY

Ubuntu is an ancient African philosophy that comes from the Zulu phrase "Umuntu ngumuntu ngabantu," which translates to, "A person can only be a person through others." The philosophy speaks to the idea that everyone's humanity is interconnected to others. Nelson Mandela, former South African leader, was a huge champion of Ubuntu and this fact was referenced by former president Barack Obama in 2013 during the eulogy for Mr. Mandela. President Obama stated that Ubuntu was

Mandela's greatest gift to the world, as he believed that all people of the world are bound by something that is invisible to the naked eye. However, it is something we can feel the strength of every day.

Ubuntu and Doc Rivers

All of you basketball fans out there probably recognize Doc Rivers as the legendary coach of the Boston Celtics. He was able to lead the Celtics to win the NBA Championship in 2008 and he credits the Ubuntu philosophy for his doing so. He believes the philosophy unified the team and turned them into a highly formidable force. To Doc Rivers, the basis of Ubuntu meant, "I can't be all I can be, unless you are all you can be ..." This concept turned the highly talented yet disparate players into a cohesive unit with a singular goal.

Doc Rivers used his rookie players to help spread the message of Ubuntu throughout the organization. It gradually caught on with everybody and the entire team began living the Ubuntu philosophy, according to Rivers. The team was even using it as their pregame chant, which took them through the regular season, postseason, and all the way to the championship. After winning, the team had the word Ubuntu etched into their championship ring.

When Doc Rivers left the Celtics for the Los Angeles Clippers in 2013, he brought the concept of Ubuntu with him. Even though he has not yet won another championship, he still credits the Ubuntu philosophy with helping him create a championship team that year. Overall, if you are making yourself and others better, you are also following the Ubuntu concept (Ryan, 2020).

What Ubuntu Can Mean to Business

When the concept of Ubuntu is applied to business, it has the potential to develop strong partnerships with the betterment of the community in mind. With this philosophy, people have the ability to be human and value the good of their community over self-interest. Based on history, this idea may be a little disrupting for some, but the main point is that we can elevate others while also building ourselves. As people, we are not required to step over others to win.

When this philosophy is applied to a larger scale, it has the potential to eradicate the obstacles to economic growth, like greed, corruption, or fraud. Based on the concept of "a person is who they are because of others," Ubuntu can be applied to business strategies that encourage the establishment of progressive partnerships and business networks.

A leadership coach can incorporate the philosophy of Ubuntu when working with their clients. Introducing these ideas can help build cohesiveness in any organization, no matter how different the team members are. This concept helped to unite business owners of varying backgrounds as it did with businesses in South Africa, where the idea came from.

Teamwork

UNCONVENTIONAL TECHNIQUES THAT MULTIPLY TEAM PERFORMANCE

Despite all of the information that exists about leadership, it is still confusing and difficult to be a leader in today's world. People are constantly changing, along with many other things, so staying on top of all of the new information is nearly impossible. Nonetheless, leadership skills are extremely important because they will turn a losing team into a winning team. It is not enough to have talented individuals in your group. These members must have someone who can lead them to victory. Unfortunately, history is riddled with stories of poor leadership bringing down large groups, family units, organizations, and even nations. To avoid such pitfalls, we will go over some unorthodox leadership techniques that are still very effective.

De-Hassle Instead of Delegate

You have probably been told many times in your life to delegate those things that do not require your full attention. These are items that can be done by someone else so that you have freedom to focus on more critical tasks. After all, isn't being a leader all about handing off tasks that you don't want to do over to someone else? That's not exactly true.

A great leader understands that the start of leadership has to do with building a strong team. When you build a team that knows what their mission is and what they have to do, you don't have to spend much time motivating them either. A good leadership technique that many successful individuals employ is hiring people who are smarter than them. It is a better strategy to make sure team members are not demotivated than it is to make sure they are motivated. This is done by clearing out as many hassles as possible that get in people's ways and block their performance. Smart and talented people do not need continuous motivation. They just need to stay motivated.

One of the greatest demotivators out there is incompetent people who slow everyone down because they are clueless about what they are doing. A leader needs to recognize that these individuals exist in their group and either get them up to speed quickly or find new people to replace them. Many organizations will hire workers simply because they want warm bodies on the floor. Unfortunately, this method becomes highly toxic because the talented employees will continually pick up the slack for the poor and unqualified team members. Eventually, this will cause them to burn out too.

When you have the right people on your team, make sure the work they are doing excites them. A big part of this has to do with your own enthusiasm, which we spoke about earlier. After developing a creative environment for your team, the next step is to take out the hassles, or demotivators. Make sure they have a good reason for why they are performing tasks because there will be many that are just tedious and there is no way around it.

As a leader, you will have to delegate tasks regularly, but in the process, you need to make sure the right job is being given to the correct individual. You should not delegate just to get annoying busywork off your plate. Overall, you need to hire talented people and provide the proper amount of support, but stay out of their way so they can get the job done.

Help Your Team With Their Strengths

This technique builds off the first one with the assumption that you hired people based on their unique skills and strengths. These skills were needed for the work you are involved in, so these employees are very valuable to your organization. Therefore, your job as a leader is to help these individuals spend a significant amount of time on their strengths. A strength is not just something we are good at, but what also gives us energy.

Determine what your team members are good at. What gives them the energy to keep moving and thriving? Once you determine this, divert the workflow to play to people's strengths. This will help you build a highly energized team.

No "Buts," "Nos," or "Howevers"

The tone of any environment is generally set by the leader in the room. If the leader is acting out of control, everyone else will feed off this energy and lose their minds, as well. Think about your first reaction to any idea. Are you optimistic or pessimistic? Are you receptive or dismissive? Do you actually hear someone out or just shut them down? Is the atmosphere you have created conducive to people feeling comfortable with speaking up? You would never want someone with a good idea to sit quietly because they are afraid of expressing it.

"A company's communication structure should not mirror its organizational structure. Everybody should be able to talk to anybody."

— ED CATMULL

No one should feel like they will be chastised or ridiculed for bringing forth an idea. Most people would agree with this assessment. Unfortunately, many individuals in managerial roles unintentionally react to new ideas in a negative way. Their reaction discourages the people who bring them up from doing so in the future. The words "no," "but," and "however" are the biggest culprits to inciting this type of reaction. Starting a sentence with any one of these words gives the message of being wrong, no matter how friendly the tone that was used.

You are not required to agree with every idea that comes your way. However, you must make people feel good for having the courage to come to you with an idea. When your first response is one of the previous words, you have effectively made the other person feel disappointed. When a person feels this way immediately, they will stop coming to you with their ideas, even if you ultimately agree with them, and even implement them.

Instead, use phrases like, "that's quite interesting," or "thanks for presenting this to me; tell me more." These phrases give some credence to the other person and their ideas.

Praise Immediately

Giving regular feedback is an essential thing a leader must provide for their team members. Top performers in any field crave feedback because they want to know how well they did and what they can do better. They are always looking to improve in any way possible. Edward Thorndike had a favorite term, which was "Law of Effect." Basically, an action that gets rewarded is also repeated more often, whether it is good or bad. So, if you reward bad behavior, people will engage in more bad behavior. When you punish an action, it will happen less often. This idea is the basis of societal laws.

This is why it's imperative to praise employees often. Of course, make sure the praise is sincere and only occurs when it's warranted. Don't just throw around praise when your employees have not earned it. However, when they do something worthy of recognition, no matter how small, praise them for it immediately. This will make them feel good and result in them doing it more often. Praise is more effective when you do it fast. If you praise someone for a positive act several days later, they may not even know what you are talking about.

It's important to keep your feedback constructive. Here are some pointers to help you out:

- Criticism is important for helping people grow. When someone needs to improve in a certain area, it's essential to provide them feedback on how to do so. However, all of your focus cannot be on criticizing. You also need to give praise when they do something well. Remember that criticism is not the same thing as being insulting.
- Praise should be specific and not general statements like "nice work." Instead, say something like "Great job on organizing the files."
- Praise or criticism should be targeted at the work and not the person. Don't make it personal.

Encouragement

Clarity Creates Efficiency

There is much psychological research that shows uncertainty leads to anxiety, which can affect decision-making. Even the smallest uncertainties lead to reduced clarity in communication. This makes tasks harder for the people you manage.

As a leader, it is your job to use as much clarity as possible when communicating. If you create any doubt in a situation, it can demotivate your employees, create unnecessary confusion, and decrease efficiency. Sometimes, even one sentence or phrase in an email can change the dynamic of what happens later on. So, make clarity of communication a continual habit. Always make your expectations known and the next step as obvious as possible. Clarity of communication is something your team will thank you for.

Hands Off

When something is going wrong, the natural reaction for many people is to jump in and fix it. However, should you always jump in and fix it? When you do it yourself, you know it will get done to your standards. The answer here might surprise you, though.

When you have risen to the role of being a leader, your job is not to make sure everything is up to your standards. That involves too much micromanaging and is just a waste of time. Your objective is to make sure the whole team gets the best possible results. Determine what the cost is to you when you get involved in every project, even when it is your expertise. Is it really worth your time to make sure it is perfect?

When your team feels micromanaged, they will stop coming up with ideas on their own. Instead of growing your team and working on new strategies, you will spend your time putting out fires. Weigh in when necessary, but let your people do the work they were tasked to do. They might make more mistakes, but as long as the job gets done sufficiently, you will still be in good shape.

Answer Questions With Questions

In order to foster an environment where people come up with their own answers, you must not tell them what to do. Instead, answer questions with questions to help guide your team members into figuring out their own solutions.

Your job as a leader is to get the best results from your team and you cannot do that if you spend your time fixing all of the problems. Everyone else in your group will need to be able to solve their own problems.

The idea here is that your team is down in the trenches. They have more information about a problem than you do, but they are just feeling overwhelmed. You can use your managing skills to help guide them, but don't give them the answer. They need you to provide them with a new perspective, and this will lead to more clarity in figuring out solutions.

When employees are treated as more than mere followers, an organization starts to thrive. When they are given the opportunity to solve their own problems, they feel more valuable to the company. Therefore, answer questions with questions whenever you can. Ask probing questions that will help them answer it themselves. Your goal is to help people realize they have the information and capability to come up with answers on their own. Once they do, they will feel empowered to do more.

Togetherness

BUILDING A STRONG TEAM AROUND YOU

"If you want to go fast, go alone. If you want to go far, go together."

— AL GORE

It is easy to move quickly when you are alone. You have no one else to worry about who can weigh you down. However, you can only go so far when you are alone. With others, your journey can be extended indefinitely as the sky becomes the limit. However, it is important to have a good team around you, otherwise, you will not only be slower, but less effective. Many self-help and motivational coaches out there promote the philosophy of having a strong inner circle. This is important because you ultimately will turn into the people you spend the majority of your time with.

If you look at almost any successful person throughout history, they had a team of people around them. Also, if you asked most of them honestly, they would tell you that they could not do it on their own. This is absolutely true. If you research some of the greatest breakthroughs throughout the world, one person generally gets the credit, but there was a whole group of people who helped make it happen. Think about some of the biggest companies in modern times, like Amazon, Tesla, Facebook, or Microsoft. The heads or founders of these companies get the media attention, but they all have a strong team unit that is helping them run their operation.

The point here is that great things are not created alone. They are done by groups of people who are on a common mission, being guided by a strong leader. In this section, we will detail some of the most common reasons to build a good team around you. Building teams is what leadership is all about.

Enhances Your Effort

Legendary football coach Vince Lombardi once stated that confidence is contagious. The same idea holds true for effort. When you are around people who are putting in a large amount of effort towards a goal, it inspires you to do the same. When the person next to you is working hard, it raises your work ethic. By the same token, when the person is being lazy, that also rubs off on you. This observation was found to be consistent whether the task they were doing was difficult, easy, or completely unrelated to yours. Work ethic alone rubbed off on people.

Other studies done in the past have found that teenagers performed better in strong teams. For example, when they had to engage in problem-solving tasks together, they engaged in more exploratory behavior and learned faster compared to working by themselves.

Social Support and Advice

"The strength of the team is the individual. The strength of the individual is the team."

— PHIL JACKSON

A team is composed of many individuals with their own unique skills and strengths. If we help maximize each person's talents, then the team becomes stronger as a whole. Having access to social support from a network of people will help each person develop their skills. These networks can also act as a stress buffer and improve coping skills. This will vastly improve your mood and well-being.

Receiving advice from people can help reduce anxiety. In many cases, we feel like we have the right answer, but are unsure of ourselves. Being able to bounce ideas off other people and receive advice from people who have been where we want to be can give us peace of mind. Of course, make sure you are getting advice from the right people. Preferably, seek out someone beyond family or close friends to get the most objective viewpoints you can.

Social support can come in many forms, whether it is advice, someone making you feel more comfortable about a situation, or a teammate allowing you to vent your frustrations. All of these are important aspects of social support. Finding individuals who can satisfy all of these needs is essential to having a good team around you. A team supports one another and has each others' back. Each member realizes that when one person is down, everyone is down and needs to lift them back up. Think of a team like a chain. If one link in the chain is broken, the entire chain becomes weak. The same holds true for members of a team.

Helps Develop Resilience

Building a strong team can help build resilience because all of the problems are not being taken on by one person. Using a support system has been found to be a key way that Olympic champions develop their resistance because a problem shared is basically a problem halved. Asking for help has long been thought to be a sign of weakness. However, the opposite is true. Asking for feedback, and using it when appropriate, is actually a hallmark of a strong and mature learner.

Enhances Motivation

Motivation is enhanced by things like having a sense of purpose, choice, mastery, personal belonging, or relatedness to a group. In a randomized control trial with university students, it was found that being part of a peer-network increased participation in physical activity. Students who had a supportive team around them were more motivated than if they simply listened to motivational messages.

Jonny Wilkinson, who is a famous rugby player, stated in his autobiography that when he gave himself to the team, he would get 15 times the support back because each player on the team would support him. Basically, within a team, what you give out is what you will get back. This realization by Mr. Wilkinson is what led him and his team to win the 2003 World Cup.

Think about various groups that you have been a part of throughout the years. These groups may have been for school, work, or various other gatherings. Ask yourself how the individuals in the group behaved and how much of that was related to the leader of that group. Were the members defiant, combative, and confrontational, or were they friendly, supportive, and helpful? How much of their behavior mirrored other members of the team, especially the leader? A leader has the ability to set the tone for how a group functions. So, if they are behaving as a leader should, they will receive the same treatment back from the group members.

Improves Your Self-View

How people talk to others greatly reflects how those individuals talk about themselves, especially when the words are coming from an authority figure of some sort. For example, an education study done on how teachers speak to their students determined that the words a teacher uses impacted how the students viewed themselves. The authors of this study figured out that positive statements made by teachers directly related to positive self-talk.

How people, in general, speak to us will impact our self-view, even when it is at a young age. Within a team, the encouragement we receive from the people around us can improve how we think about ourselves. We spoke about the importance of giving praise earlier in this chapter. Encouraging team members to praise each other is essential, especially at the top from the leader.

Helps Deal With Stressful Situations Better

Stressful situations are hard to deal with, but it becomes much more difficult when handling them on your own. Having a network of trusted individuals who you can turn to can be a very helpful way to cope with major issues. Carrying large loads on your back is overwhelming, but each person you add to help you carry that weight will be beneficial to you.

Can Improve Performance

In one of the earliest studies done in sports psychology, it was found that people worked harder when they knew other people were watching them. The same behaviors hold true in the workplace. If people know they are being watched, they will put in more effort in every respect. In a study done with over 300 participants, it was discovered that people who had deep, meaningful relationships with others saw an improvement in their work performance. Good relationships between colleagues resulted in higher trust, support, and pride in work.

Performance

All of these advantages are based on having a strong team full of helpful members who do their part. If you accidentally build a team with poor members, then you will have the opposite effect. Also, having to offer social support to people who are not holding up their end will drain all of your energy. When building a team, always get the best people you can find.

A good way to develop teams is by engaging in team-building activities and exercises that strengthen bonds between all of the members, including the leader. Leading a cohesive team will place you at the center of responsibility and teamwork. Figure out games that you can play which will require the effort of everyone in a group. A great example of this is Helium Stick, where each member has to lower a dowel rod to the group using one finger each. Games like this showcase the value each team member brings to the group and helps to break the ice between the leader and employees.

As a leader, do not expect or demand perfection from your workers. Promote the idea of taking action over that of being perfect in every way. When mistakes happen, don't dwell on them. Learn from them and move on. If you expect perfection, your employees will always be walking on eggshells, which will limit the ability of expression and free thought. If they know they don't have to be perfect at every turn, then they will feel empowered to take on more work and engage in calculated risks. We are not saying you should not expect quality work.

However, expecting something to be done without any mistakes is too much to ask of anybody.

UNDERSTANDING WHAT A GREAT TEAM IS

Teamwork!

Think about your favorite team for a moment, whether it is in sports or any other activities. These individuals will work flawlessly together, like a well-oiled machine. You might be thinking that their chemistry is so great that they automatically work well together. However, you are just witnessing the final product and not seeing all of the work that went on behind the scenes. Flawless teamwork does not just occur out of the blue. While it's true that some people naturally work better together, building a truly cohesive team takes a lot of time and continuous effort, which is needed by all members, including the leader. We will go over some essential elements that must be present for every great team.

Clear Objectives

Every member of a team must understand clearly the basis of a particular activity as it relates to the overall objective. Basically, any activity the members engage in must have a clear purpose for why they are doing it. For example, if you task an employee with writing blogs to help market your organization, they must understand why and how the blog will help the company achieve their higher objective. If they don't see the purpose, they will not be motivated to give their best performance and the project will be a failure. You will then have to pay extra funds to outsource the project.

Clear Roles

Each individual, from the leader to all employees must understand their role, so as to not cause confusion or create chaos. If people are not aware of their roles, they will step on each others' feet continuously. Therefore, every team member must be aware of the hierarchy and know what tasks they need to perform. This is not meant to be insulting, but you cannot have too many chiefs, and too few Indians, as the old expression goes.

Flawless Communication

We have mentioned communication multiple times throughout this book, and that's because it's essential to any team dynamic. Whenever someone gets an idea or has a question, they should be able to express it unencumbered. The communication must be as smooth as possible to avoid any misinformation. If there is

LET ME LEAD YOUR WAY | 95

confusion, people need to feel comfortable with speaking up and others need to be okay with clarifying information. It is better to take some extra time to ensure everyone involved is on the same page than have to deal with the consequences of miscommunication later on.

Cooperation

You may have heard the old expression that there is no "I" in the word team. Teamwork is not about promoting individual achievements, but rather about what everyone accomplishes together. Whenever you are working in a group, every member plays a role in whatever success is created. Therefore, each member should also get their fair share of the credit. Also, never boast about doing the most amount of work. A team needs to create a balance and utilize everyone's strengths appropriately. While being part of a unit, there will be days where you carry much of the load, while on other days, someone else will take on most of the work. This is common for any team environment and does not mean that people are slacking off. We all have our good days and bad days, which makes working in a team much more advantageous.

Individual Development Within the Team

Even though you are working on a team, you must be careful to not lose your independent voice. People do not form a group because everyone is the same. It is quite the opposite. The reason teams work well is because everyone is different and they all bring in their unique strengths. While working in collaboration with others, never forget about your own personal development.

Always remember these various components when it comes to building a team and you will always be on the right path.

UNITY BETWEEN TEAM MEMBERS

People change, grow, prosper, and even drift apart. A leader must always observe the members of their team to continuously evaluate how they are working together. If you have done your job as a leader, your team should be able to function mostly independent of you. This does not mean that you are not needed; however, you should also not be expected to guide your workers every step of the way. Your work is not done by forming a team and just giving orders, but rather by giving guidance so our team can collaborate with each other. From here, you will simply oversee that everything is going smoothly.

Unity

Monitor and Review

To understand if you have developed a strong team, you must use obvious metrics that will monitor the success of the team and every individual in it. These metrics can include things like finance, customer feedback, or product output. If some of these metrics are lagging, then it may be time to make changes. When you set specific goals, you must measure the achievements at precise intervals of time, like monthly, quarterly, or annually. Here are some simple questions to make the process easier for you:

- What achievements has the team made so far?
- What changes have occurred?
- What have the team members learned?
- What's working well at this time?
- Is there any friction?
- What aspects of teamwork need improvement?

There is a lot that goes into building a functioning team. This is one of the main reasons that hiring a leadership coach can be helpful. As a leader who might be struggling with developing a cohesive team, a good coach can assist in many ways.

FUN ACTIVITIES TO IMPROVE LEADERSHIP

As we mentioned earlier, leadership is not about who has the highest academic skills or went to the most prestigious schools.

We are not saying book education is not important, but it is also no guarantee for having leadership skills. Leaders are thrown into various situations and must be able to think and react quickly. They must also have the ability to problem-solve.

A great way to build leadership skills is to play games that require people to test their leadership abilities. The best way to learn is to be engaged. Therefore, fun games and activities can often be the best teachers. What's more engaging than having a good time? We will go over some games that will make you and your team members better leaders.

Pass the Hoop

With this activity, a group of people will stand in a circle and hold hands. The objective here is to pass a hula hoop around the circle without letting it touch the ground. The game involves teamwork, problem-solving, and communication. All of these are essential skills for any leader to possess.

Maneuver the Minefield

The first step is to blindfold one of your team members and set up an obstacle course around the room. The blindfolded person will have to get from one section of the room to the next without running into obstacles, or mines. Of course, do not use any dangerous obstacles that will cause injuries. Items like pillows or balloons will work well enough.

The job of the team members is to guide the individual as they move around the room. Team members can use only a limited number of words that are agreed upon at the beginning. For example, the words can be left, right, back, or forward. This game can be done almost anywhere with a big enough space. An office retreat or party is a great place to get it done. This game will improve your communication skills and trust with your team members.

Stand Up

This is a very simple activity to perform. Two individuals have to sit facing each other with the soles of their feet together. They should also be holding hands. The objective here is to stand up at the same time. This is another great way to develop teamwork, trust, problem-solving, and collaboration.

Deserted Island

This is a fun game where you have people break up into teams. Each team has to choose five items that they believe are essential for survival. Remember, it is not the items that you like, such as your favorite clothes. These items are absolutely necessary if you were to be stuck on a deserted island.

The team must come to a consensus based on collaboration and compromise. This exercise is great for learning how to work with limitations. It also involves planning, risk-taking, and proper communication. All of these are basic skills a leader must possess.

Shapeshifting

For this exercise, you will need a long rope. Take both ends and tie them together, forming a loop. The rope needs to be large enough so every member in your group can hold onto it with both hands. From here, someone will shout out a shape and the members holding the rope will create that shape with the rope and place it on the ground. After a little while, the group will stop speaking verbally, and instead, use hand gestures and other nonverbal communication methods to get the job done. This activity is great for communication and teamwork.

All of these exercises are great for developing the leadership skills required for the business world. One final activity you can do is to get into a small group and have a discussion about the leaders all of you know and admire. Describe why you admire these leaders and what qualities you can take from them. The results will be enlightening and you will bond more with your group. You may even find out that you have more in common than you think.

Now that we have detailed what leadership is and some effective ways to develop the proper skills, we will discuss more about leadership coaching.

Group activities

5

BEST QUESTIONS TO ASK WHEN COACHING LEADERSHIP

A leadership coach will not give advice or instructions. They will not tell their clients what should be done. Instead, they will guide the client in finding their own answers to get to their desired destinations. This idea is similar to a roadmap. It is up to the driver where they want to go, but the map will guide them along the way.

One of the most essential techniques to help guide a client is asking appropriate questions. In many ways, this will be the heart of any coaching session because asking appropriate questions at the right times will ultimately lead clients to the correct answers.

11 AREAS OF LEADERSHIP COACHING TO EXPLORE IN THE WORKPLACE

Important Questions

When working with clients who hold leadership roles in the workplace, there are several areas that can be explored. You can touch on these topics by asking specific questions, whether you are coaching individuals or a group of people. The goal here is to determine which areas your client needs improvement in when working with their team.

Communication

There is a wide array of channels used for communication today, including face-to-face, email, phone, video conferences, or instant messenger. Determine the core ways that a leader generally communicates. The following are some coaching questions to get into with your client in regard to communication.

- What is currently working well around your communication methods and what is not?
- In relation to your team, what are their general preferences around communication? What are your preferences around communications?
- What are the strengths that you bring to communication?
- What are some of the blind spots around your communication?
- What are some of the difficult conversations that need to occur with your team members?

Communication

Influence

Because of the matrixed team environment we are working in, many relationship boundaries are crossed on a regular basis. Even if we have no direct line of reporting with certain individuals, we may still have some type of working relationship with them. Learning to manage up and across with these people requires us to use the skill of influence. Influence means you have the ability to affect the character, development, or behavior of someone or something. The following are some questions to explore with clients in regard to influence:

- What does the concept of influence mean to you?
- What does influence look like?
- In what area of your role/team/department is influence the most important?
- What is working for you around influence and what is not?
- In your organization, who models influence well, and what can you learn from them?

Relationship Building

In a professional environment, you may be part of multiple teams and interface with a large variety of internal and external stakeholders. Even if you work in isolation, the success of your project usually involves and impacts several people. The following are some coaching questions to consider when working with your leadership client on relationship building:

- What are the key relationships you want to give the most attention to?
- What is currently working in your relationships with your team and what is not?

- What is required of you in your key relationships?
  What do your team members need the most from you?
- What is helping your key relationships thrive?
- Who models relationship-building well and what can
  you learn from them?

Team Leadership

This is a core leadership skill. Coaching sessions in team leadership may take us into various areas, like micro-monitoring rather than micro-managing, empowering others on your team, developing your team, coaching skills, and recognizing the personal needs of each of your teammates. Some coaching questions to explore with team leadership are as follows:

- What does the team need from me as the leader and
  what do they need from each other?
- What are the personal support needs of each team
  member?
- What independent and valuable skills does each team
  member bring to the group?
- What is the difference between micro-monitoring and
  micro-managing?

Program and Project Management

A growing number of leaders are managing both programs and projects. In the virtual space, where much of the work is getting done today and team members are working interdependently, skills in matrix management and teamwork can be highly beneficial. The following are some coaching questions to consider when dealing with program and project management:

- What projects are currently going on for the team?
- How are these projects being planned, monitored, and what are you learning from them?
- Which of the programs and projects require design?
- What program and project management skills, tools, and technologies need to be developed?
- What actions are being taken to keep the programs and projects done on time, within scope, and within the budget?

Meetings

In almost every company you have been involved with, there have probably been a large number of meetings with professionals at all levels. These meetings can either be informative or a complete waste of time. Since so much time is spent in these different meetings, it is beneficial to make sure they are as efficient as possible. This means you provide the most amount of information in the least amount of time, but still make sure your team members have a solid understanding of what you go over. The following are some questions to explore with clients when it comes to meetings:

- What are you currently doing to keep meetings on track? What is working well and what is not?
- What strategies will create more efficiency during your meetings? What are some of the timewasters? What will you start doing now?
- Are the right people at your table?
- What is the best type of conversation to help cover the information in meetings the best?

Presentations

Whether you are in team meetings, formal presentations, or presenting to your peers, you have to make sure your message is getting across in a way that is understandable by your audience. Otherwise, you are just wasting your breath. Unfortunately, too many professionals display their content in a way that only they are receptive to. If there is a major presentation on the horizon, the following are some coaching questions to explore so your client can get their information across more effectively:

- What are the three key bullet points of the presentation?
- How are you going to capture the people's attention right from the start? What is your hook?
- What is the call to action? What are you urging your audience to do?
- How can you make the presentation more meaningful

to your audience? What can you do to make it relatable to them?

Conflict Management

Whenever people are working across distance and time, conflict is bound to occur at some point. This is an area that many groups struggle with. As time goes on and problems get swept under the rug, the conflict slowly festers and things can ultimately blow up when any of us least expect it. As emotions soar, trust, relationships, and engagement decline. Consider these coaching questions to go over with clients to improve their conflict management skills:

- What is your current approach to dealing with conflict?
- What are some of your biggest triggers? (Lying, laziness, passive-aggressiveness, disorganization, etc.)
- What is the team's default action for conflict? What do they automatically do?
- Are there any "hot items" with the team that are boiling up? Is there anything being done to resolve these items? What actions can you start taking?
- When you start considering how to resolve conflict, what specific outcomes are you looking for? What are the important things about the relationships that you want to hold on to?

Working Across Differences

When you work with a group of people, there are going to be many differences. This includes differences in culture, background, goals, strengths, weaknesses, people skills, and how to approach life. Being able to work across these differences is the foundation of a good leader and team dynamics. As business is becoming more globalized and we have the ability to work with people all over the world, clients need to be much more skilled at developing relationships with people, no matter how different they are. Here are some questions to explore with your clients:

- When you consider the people you work with, what is important to them?
- What needs do they have that could be fulfilled at work?
- What are some of their personal preferences?
- What does the role of the team, organizational, or individual culture play?
- What adaptations need to be made to your style and approach that will make you more cohesive with your team members?

Performance Management

Providing feedback is a key component for employees today. Whether the conversations are positive or negative, they need to happen regularly. The following are some leadership questions to explore with your clients:

- What conversations need to take place?
- What are the differences between performance conversations, feedback, and difficult conversations? What are the positive and constructive points of each of these conversations?
- How good and comfortable are you with these necessary conversations? What are your strengths and weaknesses, and what can you do to develop yourself further in these areas?
- When dealing with specific conversations, what point are you trying to get across and what method is going to be best understood?
- What do you need to follow up on and when?

Coaching and Mentoring Skills

Leaders need to build up capability within their teams. It is critical for success, especially in the virtual or remote world. These capabilities can include various coaching and mentoring skills or providing peer-to-peer support. The following are some coaching questions to explore with your clients in this area:

- What are the differences between coaching and mentoring in your company?

- What different hats do you wear in building capability with your team?
- As the leader, how are you supporting others' dreams and goals? How are you holding team members accountable?
- What kind of support does your team need in building capability?

As coaches go into different organizations, the coaching needs will vary. Therefore, leadership coaches need to tailor their methods based on what their clients need. Determine which of the above areas your client needs the most help in and go from there. Use these questions as a guide.

POWERFUL COACHING QUESTIONS

Asking great questions is one of the strongest tools in a coach's arsenal. Powerful questions inspire thought, creativity, and intrigue and lead to great results for clients. When confronted with questions, leaders tend to ponder and find solutions to their problems. If you searched for powerful questions on the internet, you would find a list of millions to choose from. Here are five tested and proven questions to help your clients reach the next level:

- What does success feel like to you? This is a simple question but can promote deep thought. Many people take the idea of success for granted, but if they actually stopped to think about it, they would be surprised to learn their true thoughts. So many people are fixated on other people's view of success, instead of their own. Success is not about material things or money. The keyword here is "feel." The feeling of success is personal.

- What does this mean to you? When a client has too many interests and opportunities, this question invites them to dig deeper into their values, eliminates external influences, and connects them to their core.

- What is standing in your way? Everyone deals with challenges, and we must learn to navigate around them. If you give your clients the space to go over their obstacles, they may realize that the challenges are not as bad as they thought.

- What goals do you have for 10 years down the line? Many people only think about immediate goals that create instant gratification. However, to create long-term goals, you will need to delay gratification at times. Think of how far you have come over the last ten years. Now imagine having the same or greater amount of growth ten years from now.

- What one thing can you do right now that will move you in the right direction? This will break down your long-term goals into smaller action steps that are easier to take.

The Anatomy of a Powerful Question

There is no real script for asking a powerful question. The goal is to elicit a good response that will help both the asker and responder to learn something. Powerful questions evoke clarity and create greater possibilities. They reveal something that was not known before. As a leadership coach, you need to understand what a powerful question looks like. To give you an idea, consider the following:

- It needs to be open-ended. The answer should not be a simple yes or no but should allow for further questions to be asked. An example would be, "What steps do you plan on taking to reach this specified goal?"
- It comes from the beginner's mindset. Tell yourself that you are unaware of the answer to the question.
- It needs to be clear and succinct. Keep it simple and do not use too many words. If you need to give more context, you can always use follow-up questions to get it across.
- It needs to be impactful and stand out from the rest of the questions. Of course, in a coaching session, most questions will need to be this way.
- It needs to happen at the moment and not be rehearsed ahead of time. While coaching sessions need structure, much of the conversation will be on the spot. There are no rehearsal periods. Therefore, powerful questions cannot be rehearsed.

These questions will help your clients push beyond their limitations and increase their performance. Asking powerful questions is a skill that takes time to master. To practice, be fully present with your client at all times and listen intently to your clients. Take time to learn about asking appropriate questions. Once you become an expert in this skill, your potential as a leadership coach will become limitless.

Powerful questions

6

LEADERSHIP DEVELOPMENT SKILLS AND METHODS

We have made the distinction between being a boss and leader several times throughout the book, and for good reason. The two are not the same thing. A boss is someone who directs and instructs their employees. They are more of an authority figure. A leader is more like a colleague, or equal. They are someone who can inspire their team members. Effective leaders have a deep interest in people and enjoy helping them harness their skills so they can become more successful. A skillful team is great for business.

Business leadership coaches can help develop these leaders who will influence and create a major change for an organization. The focus of this chapter will be to learn about leadership coaching methods and skills and how you can use them. Managers within a company can also use these skills to help grow their team. Coaching skills do not only have to be used by coaches.

BUILDING GENUINE TRUST

Being genuine is a trait that is underrated. Many people act nice and pretend to care, but it is really just for show. Eventually, people will pick up on it. Likewise, people will pick up on someone being genuine, because they know that person really cares. In your daily communication with people, there may have been several conversations that were empty and meaningless. The topics that were discussed simply took up time and did not create any real connections. In essence, they were fake conversations.

With a good coach, this will not happen because they will be able to deeply connect with you. This means they are able to move beyond the superficial characteristics to understand individual strengths and weaknesses. This ability helps to build genuine trust, and in order for your team to respond to you appropriately, this type of trust is essential because it is real. After all, you are asking them to be introspective, which requires them to open up quite a bit about themselves.

A great way to build trust is by actively listening to your clients. At every moment, let them know that you are hearing what they say. Too often people are not actually listening to others to determine what they are trying to convey. Instead, they are simply waiting to respond. In order to actively listen, you must fully concentrate on what is being said. Take note anytime conversations are happening and summarize the points made by a client back to them. This ensures that all parties are on the same page. These techniques will show that you are genuinely interested in what your client has to say and have a vested interest in helping them out.

Unfortunately, many leaders lack this essential skill. If you want to be a successful coach, whether as a side gig or business, active listening skills are a must. The following are a few simple steps to turn you into a better listener:

- Pay attention to what is being said by giving the speaker your undivided attention. Look directly at them, put aside distracting thoughts, avoid preparing a rebuttal ahead of time, and pay attention to body language. A large part of communication is nonverbal.
- Show them that you are listening by portraying proper body language and gestures. Make good eye contact, nod occasionally, keep a good posture that is open, and encourage the speaker to continue with approving verbal comments.
- Provide feedback and follow-up questions to gain more clarity. This will show that you are trying to understand the person completely.
- Avoid interrupting the speaker, because they will just become frustrated. Do your best to wait for a pause

before you start speaking. If you must interrupt, do so politely and then allow the person to get back to the conversation.

- Respond appropriately by being candid, open, and honest. It is okay to assert your opinions, but do it respectfully. Treat the person as you would want someone to treat you.

Practice the skill of active listening as often as possible and it will soon become natural for you. Remember the old saying that there's a reason people were born with two ears and only one mouth. When you speak, you are repeating what you know. When you listen, you are learning something you did not know.

DEMONSTRATE EMOTIONAL INTELLIGENCE

Along with active listening skills, emotional intelligence is an essential skill that coaches must possess. It is easy to make observations about an employee, like when they don't speak up in meetings, miss important calls, or don't respond to emails. They might even miss out on great business opportunities that they were looking forward to.

The average person would look at all of this and chalk it up to laziness. An emotionally intelligent person would think something much deeper is going on. They would try to get to the heart of what's going on. Coaches who have emotional intelligence are able to put themselves in the shoes of a team member and understand their personal struggles. They will get to the heart of why that individual is behaving in the manner that they do. Are they really just being lazy or is there some underlying fear going on? From here, a coach can start identifying solutions because they know what a person is going through. With that kind of understanding, it's easier to devise effective strategies to start overcoming barriers to success. This is probably the most important role a coach has.

Many people who are successful in the professional world say that emotional intelligence, which is known as EQ, is more critical than the intelligence quotient, or IQ. Being smart is important, but understanding people will take you to the next level.

Building Emotional Intelligence

If you have never operated with much emotional intelligence, then it's important to start building up this quality for your coaching practice. Furthermore, it's important to be emotionally intelligent as a leader because you will need to understand your team members on a deeper level before you can start helping them. We will go over several essential ways to become more emotionally intelligent. The following are some of the qualities that are essential to adopt:

- Utilize an assertive style of communicating. This does not mean you are rude, loud, or obnoxious. Assertiveness simply means that you communicate your needs in a direct and confident manner. You are clear about what you want and don't back down. At the same time, you are showing respect to the other person.

- Respond instead of reacting to conflict. When a conflict arises, it is common to become emotionally overwhelmed and have outbursts of sadness or anger. These reactions can have negative consequences and we end up regretting such decisions or impulses. An emotionally intelligent person stays calm during the conflict and avoids making impulsive decisions. The goal during times of conflict is resolution, and making conscious choices that are well thought-out is important. An emotionally intelligent person will always understand that.

- They use active listening skills. Where have we heard that before? We won't revisit this whole topic again, but just know that emotional intelligence and active listening are tied together.

- They motivate themselves constantly. They set proper goals and are resilient in the face of challenges.

- Emotionally intelligent people are aware of the moods of the people around them. They remain guarded about these emotions because they understand that negativity is contagious.

- They are self-aware, which means they recognize their emotions and how they affect those around them. They are also good at picking up the feelings and nonverbal cues of those around them so they can use that information to boost their communication skills.

- Being able to take critique well is important for emotional intelligence. Instead of getting offended, a person with EQ will try to understand the criticism and see if it is valid. Being a coach or a client means that criticism will be thrown your way and you must be able to handle it and use it in your favor.

- Like a true leader, an emotionally intelligent person sets high standards for themselves and sets an example for others. They take initiative and have great problem-solving and decision-making skills.

- Finally, emotionally intelligent people come off as approachable. This does not mean you have to be the most talkative person in the world. However, people must feel like they can come up to you and speak honestly.

MOTIVATE, DON'T DEMOTIVATE

During high-pressure situations, leadership roles can move more towards a directive approach. Rather than motivating others, this change can actually have the opposite effect. As a coach, it is important to take time to recognize how you are viewed by your peers. Do you come off as approachable and inspiring, or more like an authoritarian? The difference here is that one can be motivating while the other is demotivating. Are you approachable like you think you are?

An important action for a coach and leader is to assess what drives your individual team members. What motivated them to keep working? Is it their families, money, the ability to travel, or having freedom? Once you determine this, figure out ways to incorporate these drivers into your coaching plan.

By doing this, you are changing a person's thought process. Instead of waking up and only thinking about the grueling tasks that need to be done, they are thinking about the real reason they are putting in the work every day. Essentially, they are thinking about their "why," as in, "why am I doing this?" Remembering your "why" is very powerful and will keep people motivated, even through the most difficult times. Intrinsic motivation skills are highly valuable for both individual and team performance.

LEAD ACCOUNTABILITY

Let's face it. If you have a discussion with someone and they say they will do something, in many instances, they will not. This is a quality that many people possess and there are many excuses for why this occurs. One of the main reasons is lack of time. However, the truth is that there's a lack of accountability. A person can say they will do something all they want, but if no one holds them accountable, they will just talk and provide no action.

As a coach, if you do not hold your clients accountable, the long discussions you have about improvements, incentives, and future plans will have little to no impact. You will basically have a session where you map out a great plan, only to realize nothing was followed through on. Many coaches and leaders believe that they have provided much clarity in their discussions with team members. While what they said may have been clear, it may also have lost its effect the moment a meeting is over.

A helpful exercise during sessions is to make sure everything is recorded. Having a notebook to write down the discussion topics and plans for the future should be written down. This way, coaches, leaders, and team members can visually see and remember what needs to be done. Any goal should have action steps and deadlines written down with them. It's important to check the progress of what was written down on a regular basis.

In today's age, you do not need to have a notepad as you can put things down digitally. However, evidence has shown that writing something down physically helps people retain it in their memory much better.

COACH WITH PASSION

This may sound pretty obvious, but many coaches do not go into coaching because they have a passion for it, and if they did, it was lost somewhere along the way. We can tell you now that if your sole reason for getting into coaching is money, you should stay away from the field. When your motivation is financial, you will never be happy and never be effective. You must go in with the desire to help people.

Good business skills do not automatically lead to good leadership coaching, just like having knowledge does not make someone a good teacher. The goal is to be able to parlay that knowledge successfully on to others and inspire them to achieve their goals.

Great coaches are passionate about their subject and helping their clients understand it. If you are not motivated as a coach, you can expect those you are working with to not be motivated either. As a result, your team's success will be doomed.

Ask yourself the following questions:

- What are you passionate about in the workplace?
- What are you typically doing when you lose track of time?

DEVELOP LEARNING CYCLES

A good leader or coach understands that the learning process is never over. No matter how much experience you gain in any industry, there is always something new to learn. Once you stop educating yourself, you stop growing. Therefore, you need to continually learn new coaching strategies as demographics in the workplace and around the world continue to change.

Old-school coaching techniques may not work well in a modern-day setting. In addition, there are several new ways to communicate and interact with people. To develop and enhance your coaching skills, talk to newer coaches in the field and see what methods they use. You might be surprised at what you can learn. Also, you can take new classes and get certifications to improve your knowledge. These credentials will raise your credibility too.

Remember that anyone can hang up a sign and call themselves a leadership coach, or any other type of coach. This is a challenge that comes with being in a largely unregulated field. However, bad coaches get exposed quickly. To become exceptional, which should be the goal, you must develop the many attributes discussed in this chapter and throughout the book so far. Our hope is that you strive to become the best you can be.

MAKING MANAGERS BETTER COACHES

Leadership coaches who go into an organization have the ability to change the dynamics of the environment. This will be very valuable to the company, as a whole. However, what happens when the coach is no longer there? Does the team suddenly start to fall apart again? No, of course not. One of the things a leadership coach needs to do is create good leaders that already exist within an organization. Mainly, these are individuals in management or supervisory roles.

Many managers are good at what they are trained to do, which is managing the various processes of a company. They can be great at creating budgets, making sure tasks are done in a timely manner, and ensuring that everything is running smoothly as far as operations go. The problem is that managers often forget that they are working with people. As a leader, you are not leading organizations, but the people who are involved.

Therefore, leadership coaches need to work on building up managers so they begin to understand human beings and not just operations. Basically, they need to help managers become good coaches. This is done by helping them understand their team members. They need to determine what makes each individual unique, based on what they like, dislike, fear, or get joy out of, etc.

Organizations often create a vision for their future. This is a great thing to do, but the problem is, the vision often does not incorporate the workers. A better approach to take is asking team members what their goals are and trying to incorporate them into the company's vision.

Another item to consider is language. What a person says and how they say it makes a large impact on how others perceive them. Team members can become highly turned off by language that is used towards them. This means that your words carry a lot of weight and managers need to be careful about how they are used. For example, some individuals make derogatory jokes or become condescending without even realizing it. All of this can be off-putting and drive your team members away. So, as a coach, you need to assist managers in becoming more aware of their language. It can make the difference between a poor and effective leader.

Finally, managers need to become good at conflict resolution. Whenever you have a group of people working together, conflict is bound to arise, even if these individuals get along most of the time. Many conflicts are small and can be taken care of quickly without the manager even getting involved. However, unresolved conflicts lead to frustration, discontent, and a decrease in a company's performance.

Conflicts usually come about because of a lack of appreciation or autonomy. In regards to autonomy, workers feel undervalued if their managers are always hovering over them and never giving them any space. As a manager, you need to trust your team members to a certain degree and only jump in when absolutely necessary. Also, showing honest appreciation towards your team members will result in them reciprocating the same attitude.

When managers develop coaching skills, great things begin to happen for a corporation. We will now go over some coaching strategies to help managers drive their teams' success. These will truly help build your management repertoire.

Know Your Employees

You must know the employees on your team to be a great manager. We don't mean asking superficial questions, but actually getting to know them on a deeper level. Learn as much as you can about their strengths and weaknesses. Consider having all of your team members complete self-evaluations and use the information obtained to make sure you are taking advantage of each individual's strengths appropriately. Self-evaluations will usually provide more personal information than general personality tests.

Foster Transparency

If employees are not willing to open up because they are afraid, they will never build a strong team dynamic. A good way to foster transparency is for a manager to be transparent themselves. This will lead to more open communication and build trust, form relationships, and make sure everyone is on the same page. As a manager, ask yourself the following questions:

- How often do I open myself up to other people and let them get to know me better?
- Are my team members aware of my real values and motivations?
- Are the decisions and choices I make clear and consistent?
- When I make a mistake, do I own up to it with my team members?

Before you can expect your team members to open up, you must lead by example and do it yourself on a regular basis. Transparency does not mean you have to tell all of your deepest and darkest secrets. You certainly have the right to privacy. However, whatever you can reveal about yourself, it is a good idea to do so. This is especially true of fear, strengths, weaknesses, and concerns related to the team.

Collaboration Is Key

Human beings are naturally competitive. Even if they are not in a competitive environment, they will innately look at others and try to outdo them in some way. Competing in an office environment happens frequently. Competition can be good to a certain degree, but unhealthy levels can lead to backstabbing, manipulation, poor team dynamics, and a lot of distrust. All of these issues are cancerous in a team setting. It is more appropriate to encourage collaboration and recognize group achievements, rather than individual success. This will foster a culture of teamwork that thrives and members will be willing to rely on each other. A team can go much further together than a single person all by themselves.

Create Clear Objective and Goals

Strategic planning is necessary for defining clear objectives and goals. Have your team get together and start with big-picture thinking. Encourage all of them to brainstorm different ways to meet long-term goals. This is the perfect time to draw from individual strengths and ask for the team's dedication, commitment, and creativity.

Once the larger goals are recognized and defined, it is time to produce action steps to achieve them. A popular method is to break down your larger goals into smaller benchmarks and milestones. Create appropriate deadlines and make sure everyone is held accountable for them. Assess your team's cohesiveness, progression, and accomplishments along the way.

Celebrate Success

Do not wait until a goal is fully reached to celebrate. Reaching small benchmarks and milestones are also accomplishments that need to be recognized. Use these moments to celebrate group and individual success. Recognizing work anniversaries, promotions, professional gains, personal achievements, completing projects on time, and various employee wins are powerful tools for increasing team motivation and morale.

Build Mutual Trust

Effective relationships of any kind need to have a level of trust which is balanced. Once this trust is lost, the relationship will deteriorate. We spoke about fostering transparency earlier, which is effective in establishing trust. It is also good to have an open-door policy, be friendly, always communicate clearly and honestly, and be non-judgmental during any sessions or meetings. Make a strong effort to show your employees that you genuinely care about them and that you have a vested interest in their success. This will make your team feel like they are valuable.

Pave the Way for Success

You must lay the groundwork for your team's success if you expect them to achieve it. Always make sure your team has proper access to training, resources, equipment, strategies, and anything else they need to be successful at their job, within reason. If you are holding your team accountable for creating success, you must also hold yourself accountable, as well. If you notice something lacking, fix the problem as soon as possible.

Share Constructive Feedback

Constructive feedback has the potential to make or break the success of a team. Always be candid about what your employees have done well, what needs to improve, and what has not worked at all. Always remember to craft your message carefully so that it is honest without being disrespectful.

Make sure to be open to feedback from others. The best coaches are coachable themselves. When you have discussions with your employees, make sure it is not one-sided. When providing feedback, always ask if they have suggestions for you too. During discussions, keep your mind open, remain flexible, and maintain perspective.

Employees who lack proper leadership will falter when it comes to achieving team or organizational objectives. On the other hand, when team members fully understand what is expected of them, the company will be in a better position for long-term success.

THE IMPORTANCE OF EMPATHY

Empathy is a powerful quality that means having the ability to understand and share the feelings and emotions of another person. This trait is essential to building up a relationship, which any type of coach must be able to do. If you cannot develop a relationship with your client, you will never get through to them. Not only that, they will never open up and be completely honest with you.

Empathy goes much deeper than sympathy. A person who has this quality can often physically feel what another person is going through, to the point it feels like it's happening to them.

Empathy is partly innate, which means some people are naturally more empathetic than others. However, this does not mean a person cannot develop this skill later in life. If you want to become a good leadership coach, you will have to become a more empathetic person, if you are not already. Ultimately, it is not about you, but the client. The following are some strategies you can use to strengthen your own empathy:

- Challenge yourself every day. Undertaking challenges will push you beyond your comfort zone. As a result, you will gain humility, which is a key enabler of empathy. There are many ways you can challenge yourself. You just have to do something you've never done or are uncomfortable with. For example, you can learn a new skill, start a new hobby, or do something risky.

- Get out of your familiar environment and go travel somewhere. Go to a place you have never been to before. This will give you a greater appreciation for different people and cultures.

- Ask for feedback from close friends and family about your relationship skills. Ask for suggestions on improvement and check in with them periodically to see how you are doing.

- Read literature and watch movies that explore personal relationships and emotions. This technique will help you learn how to feel for other people. Many medical schools use this strategy to build up empathy for their medical students.

- Walk in other people's shoes. Ask those around you how they perceived an experience that you both shared. For example, maybe both of you watched the same movie but got something completely different out of it.

- Every one of us has hidden biases that cloud our judgment. These biases will inhibit our ability to listen and empathize. Many times, these are centered around something visible, like race, gender, or body structure (being overweight or too skinny).

- Cultivate your sense of curiosity by trying to learn something new every day. Never overlook the idea that you can learn from everybody, even if the person is young and inexperienced.
- Ask more thoughtful and provocative questions.

As you increase your empathy, you will become a more impactful coach. In every session with a client, you must be able to feel what they are going through before you can help them create a solution.

CREATING VULNERABILITY

The relationship between a coach and their client is an important bond, and in order for it to work well, vulnerability needs to be shown on both sides. Many people view vulnerability as weakness. They feel that true strength comes from being stoic and holding everything in. The reality is, true courage is shown through vulnerability because you are putting yourself out there with the potential of being harmed.

Think about it this way: If you stay inside your house, you will more likely be safe. However, you are missing out on what the world has to offer simply because you are too afraid to go out. When you walk outside your front door, you are opening yourself up to many possibilities, both good and bad. The same holds true for your feelings and emotions. When you let your emotions out, there is a possibility you will get hurt. However, you may also learn something new or get the help you need.

During a coaching session, a coach must have the ability to bring out the vulnerability of their clients. First, the coach has to set an example by being vulnerable themselves. The feeling you get from being vulnerable will be amazing and it will also be reciprocated by the client. This will catapult the relationship to another level. We will go over some more strategies that can help another person be more vulnerable with you.

Show Them You Are Trustworthy

Your client needs to feel safe when they are sharing secrets with you. At some point, they will trust you enough to share things that they don't tell their closest friends and family members. This trust needs to be taken very seriously. When your clients are telling you something, you must assure them that the conversation will never leave the room.

Always offer support and kindness to make people feel more comfortable during coaching sessions. It is difficult to open up and share deep feelings with people. So, when your client has finally opened up to you, make sure not to break this trust.

Reinforce Your No Judgment Zone

Having a fear of judgment is a major blockade to becoming vulnerable. Your clients will never want to be open with you if they always feel like you are judging them. Many of these fears stem from a person's past. If they had negative relationships where they always felt like they were being judged, it will be hard for them to ever believe anything different.

While you cannot do anything about a person's past, you can reassure them that there is no need to fear judgment from you.

Don't Pressure Them

When a person feels pressure to share their feelings, they will usually become more closed off. They will even start to feel unsafe, which is disastrous for a coach and client relationship. Patience is the key here and if you don't show it, you will just add more stress to the relationship. As a coach, allow your client to open up on their own time, and support them along the way.

GETTING CERTIFIED

While you do not need certification to become a coach, having some type of credentials makes you more attractive in the public eye. The international coaching federation (ICF) is the most well-known credentialing body for aspiring life coaches of any kind. To become certified with this group, you will need at least 60 hours of applied training and must commit to continued development. The following are some of the core competencies needed for the ICF to get certified by them.

Professional Foundations

This refers to the coach's ability to meet professional standards, ethical guidelines, and establish a coaching agreement. No matter what type of coach an individual is, they must understand the limitations of their practice and convey these to their clients. This way, a client will not confuse coaching with therapy, consulting, or advising. A coach must also define set parameters for their continued relationship with clients.

Relationship Co-Creation

It is essential for all coaches to develop trust and professional closeness with their clients. Limitations need to be placed to avoid any psychological or safety issues down the line. A coach must be able to provide support while also respecting boundaries.

Promoting Learning and Outcomes

To help clients move towards getting results, they may need to shift a client's perspective or help them reach a new level of understanding. This involves creating awareness in the client about circumstances, emotions, and perspectives where a client's perceived barriers are not grounded in reality. A coach can help clients plan goals and develop action plans that will lead them towards their desired outcome.

Effective Communication

We have already discussed this at length in this book, but just be aware that the ICF looks at effective communication as one of their core competencies.

Effective Goal-Setting

Helping clients design appropriate goals is an important technique for coaches to possess. This involves tapping into a person's values that they hold dear and transforming them into solid commitments.

Providing Feedback and Support

The support a coach is able to provide will help build up their client's efficacy, sense of competence, and self-esteem.

Encouraging a Growth Mindset

Coaches should come to their own sessions with a growth mindset so they can be an example for their clients. By supporting this mindset in your clients, you can enhance their motivation to improve their capabilities.

Developing Resilience

Life will knock everyone down at some point. It is important for people to be resilient and bounce back from failure. Coaches can help their clients develop resilience, which will encourage them to persevere and overcome many challenges.

Be aware of these and other competencies the ICF will be looking for. If you are planning to become a leadership coach or any other type of coach, then getting certified with the ICF is a good step to take. Like it or not, the public loves to see a person's credentials, and having certification through the ICF can provide a lot of credibility for you.

I hope you found these coaching methods and strategies helpful throughout this chapter. Ultimately, it will come down to how your client views you, but much can be done to create a positive perception.

Now, we will finish out this book by discussing mindset coaching.

7

THE MINDSET COACH

We hope that you have enjoyed all of our coaching books thus far, including this one. We are not done yet, as we plan on creating another book about mindset and mindset coaching in the near future. We expect that book to be just as informative as the ones we have already put out. This final chapter will give you a small preview of what will be discussed in the next book.

WHAT IS A MINDSET COACH?

The objective of coaching is to help people shift from their current position to where they want to end up. A coach can help their clients achieve their goals by:

- Helping them get clear about what they want out
  of life

- Reviewing where they are right now and how they got
  there; What worked well for them in the past and
  what didn't?

- Coming up with specific action steps to reach an
  end goal

- Coming to a consensus on a plan that works for
  everyone

These are some of the basic steps that all coaches generally follow. What makes mindset coaching unique is that these coaches also help their clients uncover the beliefs, mental blocks, behaviors, habits, and thought processes that prevent them from living the life they want to have, whether personal, professional, relational, or health-related.

A mindset coach can use a range of techniques to change the way a person thinks so that those obstacles that have been stopping them from succeeding are no longer a factor. After working with a mindset coach, a client will obtain faster and more meaningful results. They will also have more long-lasting success. Many people do not realize how much of an effect their mindset has on them, but it plays a huge role in what type of life one has.

Mindset coaches are skilled in a wide range of neuroscience-based and therapeutic techniques, like neuro-linguistic programming, Time Line Therapy, cognitive behavior therapy, and hypnosis. Energy practices like the Emotional Freedom Technique and energy alignment may also be in their wheelhouse.

All of this is on top of their existing knowledge in traditional coaching strategies like we mentioned above. Because of all these techniques a mindset coach has at their disposal, they can easily apply them toward shifting an individual's perception, changing their mind, and ultimately, altering the course of their lives.

Why Do People Trust Mindset Coaches?

People have specific goals and desires in life, but they are not always able to fulfill them. Moreover, they cannot understand why. Because of this, they will approach a mindset coach for help. These individuals are usually at the end of their rope because they feel as though they've tried everything and nothing works.

Clients who need mindset coaches are often overwhelmed with all of the potential directions they could go in. They might also be procrastinating because they lack confidence in taking proper action.

A common finding among clients of mindset coaches is that there is a disconnect with what they desire at the conscious level and what their unconscious beliefs, patterns, habits, and programming is telling them. On the surface, they are telling themselves they want something, but their unconscious mind is doing everything to prevent it from happening. For example, a person might say they want to get into shape, but they are not exercising, eating properly, or engaging in other healthy habits to make their desire a reality.

A mindset coach has the ability to unlock these unconscious patterns and work with their clients to remove them. Once these negative patterns are gone, they can be replaced with new ones that help the client move forward to achieve their goals more quickly and easily than before. Once you tap into your mindset, you will be amazed at how much you have been holding yourself back.

The truth is, there are reasons why some people achieve more than others and it comes back to mindset. Simply put, how you think, feel, and believe about a situation plays a huge role in how you get through it.

Let's discuss an example of how a mindset coach will take an approach to help a client compared to a traditional coach. If a certain individual was looking for a new job and tried many different ways of getting one, a traditional coach may help the individual find more options to find a job, like uncovering more websites or fixing up their resume. A mindset coach, on the other hand, will delve deeper and try to uncover why the person has not been able to find a new job. Perhaps the individual has:

- Limiting beliefs: Not being good enough, talented

enough, or smart enough; does not think they deserve a new job; is too old to start over

- Behaviors: Are they following up with companies? Have they applied at enough places, or did they give up after a few rejections?
- Emotions: When applying for a new job, does the client get feelings saying they are not worthy of it?

A mindset coach can uncover a lot about a person and what is holding them back.

Will Mindset Coaching Work for You?

This is a common and legitimate concern that many people have. It is important to vet your coaches to the best of your ability, as we mentioned earlier, about finding the right leadership coach. After finding a good coach who will do their part, the rest is up to you. Mindset coaching will work for you if you are willing to make positive and permanent changes in your life. If you are not ready for this, mindset coaching will be pointless. If you have already made it to this point with this book, we suspect you are willing to embrace the coaching process.

During a mindset coaching session:

- You'll be asked to think about yourself and any major relationships in an unfamiliar way.
- You will also be asked to think about situations and personal events in a different way.

- You will be expected to challenge some long-held beliefs that have been holding you back and be asked to change them.
- You will be expected to step up to the plate and take real action to achieve your goals.
- You will have to accept what happened in your past and move away from it. You will be expected to focus on your future from that point on.

Consider a few more factors if you want to know if mindset coaching will work for you:

- Are you feeling stuck in your life and ready to move forward?
- Do you have limiting beliefs or recurring thoughts of failure that are keeping you from achieving your goals?
- Do you know what you want, but have no idea how to start moving in that direction?
- Have you lost your momentum and need to get it back?
- Are you ready to take massive action to make your dreams a reality?
- Do you want to discover your purpose in life and gain clarity about your current reality?

There are different mindsets that people have. A growth mindset is needed to achieve the ultimate success in life and business. It does not matter how talented you are, how much experience you have, or how good your strategy is if you do not have the mindset to pull it all off. Research done at the Carnegie Institute showed that how a person thinks about themselves carries much more weight than any other quality they have (Gilbert, 2019). When you work with a mindset coach, you will begin accelerating in every area of your life.

Mindset coaching is definitely not for people who are happy living with the status quo. You must be ready to perform beyond anything you ever did before. Remember that coaching is an investment you make in yourself. What you decide to put in is what you will get back. Your mindset will be your biggest enabler to make changes in every area of your life. We will uncover much more about this in our next book. We hope you are as excited as we are!

CONCLUSION

First of all, everyone here at Elvin Coaches wants to thank you, the reader, for using your valuable time to read our latest book, *Let Me Lead Your Way*. This is the third book in our life coaching series and our hope is that you learned what you wanted to about leadership coaching and will pursue it both as a client and coach. Coaching is a passion that we live for every day, and the more people we can get excited about the field, the more pride we gain.

As a group, we have coached thousands of clients throughout our many years and have also inspired many individuals to become coaches themselves. If you are excited about becoming a leadership coach, you are definitely on the right track.

We started this book off by discussing the basics of leadership coaching and how it might differ from other coaching specialties, like business coaching, spiritual coaching, or general life coaching, all of which we discussed in our first two books. Leadership coaching is an effective way to produce individuals who are sorely needed in our world: leaders. Whether it is in the business world or outside world, leaders are needed to influence change and make everything around them better.

Leaders have the ability to build teams that will make a cohesive effort towards a common goal. The objective of a leader is to make sure their team members learn to rely on them as little as possible. They can do this by inspiring and motivating their teammates to work with each other. A good leader has the ability to relate to his or her followers in a positive way and interact with them like real people. At the same time, they can hold them accountable to produce their best work.

If you look throughout time, it was the people who stepped up and were willing to lead, whether they were ready or not, who were able to change the course of history. While some people used their skills to lead people astray, others used it to effect positive change, and that is what we like to focus on at Elvin Coaches. There are many unique qualities that leaders must possess if they want to influence people. It is not just about being the loudest or most dominant person in the room. A true leader knows how to inspire others, no matter what their status is.

Always remember that the actions of a leader do not have an isolated effect. Many of their decisions will ultimately impact those around them, as well. This makes their decision-making process even more crucial.

Since leaders are so important, we need to create more of them. However, the ones that we create have to be impactful. There are plenty of poor leaders out there with no real leadership capabilities. We need to change this phenomenon by promoting leadership coaching. Leadership coaches have the proper techniques, strategies, and temperament to build up new and present leaders to be the best they can be.

If you are a leader or want to become one, it is wise to seek out a leadership coach. Despite what you may hear, hiring a coach is not a luxury. The talents of a great coach can alter the course of your reality almost immediately. You just need to make sure you hire the right coach who is a good fit for you. There are definitely bad leadership coaches out there and you want to make sure not to spend more time with them than necessary. Even if you have heard great things about a coach, it does not mean they are right for you. A proper vetting process is crucial.

Just like any other type of coach, a leadership coach will not tell you what to do. Rather, they will provide guidance, like a roadmap. In the end, you will come up with your own solutions based on the answers you have inside of you, which is very empowering.

One of the most powerful tools in a coach's arsenal is their ability to ask great questions. These questions serve to give direction to a client and help them reach the right answers based on what they need. Questions should always be open-ended and exploratory. Coaches will also answer your questions with their own questions, always throwing the ball back to your court.

If you decide to become a coach someday, it is important to work on your questioning skills. You will be able to help a lot of clients in this manner. The types of questions we went over in this book are a good starting point.

We ended this book by briefly discussing what mindset coaching is, which will be the topic of our next book. For now, understand that your mindset is either holding you back or allowing you to perform at your highest level.

Having arrived at the end of *Let Me Lead Your Way*, you now need to decide how you want to proceed. Now that you have the tools and knowledge about leadership coaching, go out there and experience it yourself. Hook up with a good leadership coach and see for yourself how beneficial the practice is in creating great leaders. Once you have experienced coaching from the client's perspective, we hope that you will be even more inspired to enter the field. We need more leadership coaches in this world who are passionate about helping others.

We want as many people out there to learn about leadership coaching and benefit from the information we have provided. If you found this book useful, we encourage you to leave a favorable review on Amazon, which will help more people learn about our coaching philosophies. Our objective is to reach out and inspire as many people as possible. Thank you again, from all of us at Elvin Coaches, for taking the time to read our special book!

Good luck!

REFERENCES

Allen, T. (2019, November 20). *Do These 5 Things If You Want A Career As An Executive Coach*. Forbes. https://www. forbes.com/sites/terinaallen/2019/11/20/do-these-5-things-if-you-want-a-career-as-an-executive-coach/?sh=2ad6b94c1cbe

Baum, I. (2018, January 3). *9 Little Ways To Help Your Partner To Be More Vulnerable With You*. Bustle. https://www.bustle. com/p/9-little-ways-to-help-your-partner-to-be-more-vulnerable-with-you-7775576

Behr, J. (2020, September 14). *5 Ways Organizations Can Get the Most out of an Executive Coach*. Harvard Business Review. https://hbr.org/2020/09/5-ways-organizations-can-get-the-most-out-of-an-executive-coach

Bennett, V. (2020, April 23). *Why high performers need leadership coaching more than anyone*. Next Evolution Performance. https://nextevolutionperformance.com/2020/04/why-high-performers-need-leadership-coaching-more-than-anyone/

Berlinsky-Schine, L. (n.d.). *Why Leadership Coaching Is Essential to Your Career Development.* Fairygodboss.com. Retrieved November 27, 2020, from https://fairygodboss.com/career-topics/leadership-coaching-benefits

Bradberry, T. (2016, July 19). *8 Secrets Of Great Communicators.* Forbes. https://www.forbes.com/sites/travisbradberry/2016/07/19/8-secrets-of-great-communicators/?sh=2a48479e3029

Britton, J. (2019, April 19). *Leadership Coaching: 11 Focus Areas, Plus Coaching Questions | by Jennifer Britton MES, CHRP, CPT, PCC | The Launchpad - The Coaching Tools Company Blog.* The Coaching Tools Company. https://www.thecoachingtoolscompany.com/leadership-coaching-more-important-than-ever-11-focus-areas-plus-questions-jennifer-britton/

CMOE. (2019, February 25). *10 Effective Coaching Strategies to Help Drive Your Team to Success.* CMOE. https://cmoe.com/blog/10-effective-coaching-strategies-help-drive-team-success/

Domanski, J. (2013). *Top 10 Traits Of Great Coaching | Coaching | Mentor | Coaching Mentoring | How To Be A Mentor | Mentor Program | International Institute of Direc-*

tors and Managers | IIDM - IIDM Global. Iidmglobal.com. https://www.iidmglobal.com/expert_talk/expert-talk-categories/leadership/coach_mentor/id42522.html

Elias, B. (2018, June 5). *7 Unconventional Leadership Techniques the Multiply Your Team's Performance.* https://www.activecampaign.com/blog/leadership-techniques

Evercoach by Mindvalley. (2019a, February 6). *5 Coaching Questions That Always Work When Coaching Leaders - YouTube.* Www.Youtube.com. https://www.youtube.com/watch?v=V5PSJ1FZdko&t=24s

Evercoach by Mindvalley. (2019). *Coaching Skills for Managers to Coach Their Teams better.*

Fries, K. (2018, February 8). *8 Essential Qualities That Define Great Leadership.* Forbes. https://www.forbes.com/sites/kimberlyfries/2018/02/08/8-essential-qualities-that-define-great-leadership/?sh=2c57c5403b63

Gilbert, S. (2019, May 14). *WHAT IS A MINDSET COACH? - YouTube.* Www.Youtube.com. https://www.youtube.com/watch?v=LNLASBU3NfI

Gounis, V. (2018, September). *What is Leadership Coaching?* Bts.com. https://www.bts.com/blog-article/business-insight/what-is-leadership-coaching

Insala. (2019, February 15). *Why Is Leadership Coaching Important? The 5 Key Benefits.* Www.Insala.com. https://

www.insala.com/blog/why-is-leadership-coaching-important-the-5-key-benefits

Kiner, M. (2018, August 8). *6 Ways to Get the Most Out of a Leadership Coach | Glassdoor*. Glassdoor Blog. https://www.glassdoor.com/blog/leadership-coach/

Kruse, K. (2013, April 9). *What Is Leadership?* Forbes. https://www.forbes.com/sites/kevinkruse/2013/04/09/what-is-leadership/?sh=5a7649135b90

Landau, P. (2018, September 13). *The 9 Best Leadership Games for Skill Development*. ProjectManager.com. https://www.projectmanager.com/blog/the-9-best-leadership-games

Mindvalley. (n.d.). *The Ultimate Guide to Leadership Coaching*. Evercoach - By Mindvalley. Retrieved November 19, 2020, from https://www.evercoach.com/ultimate-guide-to-leadership-coaching/what-is-leadership-coaching

Moore, C. (2019, September 25). *32+ Coaching Skills and Techniques for Life Coaches & Leaders*. PositivePsychology.com. https://positivepsychology.com/coaching-skills-techniques/

Pexels. (2000). *Free stock photos · Pexels*. Pexels.com; Pexels. https://www.pexels.com/

Pixabay. (2018). *Pixabay*. Pixabay.com. https://pixabay.com/

Prentice, W. C. H. (2014, August). *Understanding Leadership.* Harvard Business Review. https://hbr.org/2004/01/understanding-leadership

RTC. (2018, January 29). *Coaching Techniques for Leadership Success | 6 Tips From RTC.* RTC Leadership & Coaching. https://www.rtcleadership.com/coaching-skills/6-coaching-techniques-leadership-success/

Ryan, M. (2020, September 22). *The Playbook: Why Doc Rivers Says Ubuntu Led Him and the 2008 Celtics to an NBA Title.* Www.Yahoo.com. https://www.yahoo.com/lifestyle/playbook-why-doc-rivers-says-072245595.html?guccounter=1&guce_referrer=aHR0cHM6Ly93d3cuZ29vZ2xlLmNvbS8&guce_referrer_sig=AQAAAGH1de9lRSb35lovsfBgh0Q7PmbDL9WyFomFuBcpl65BGXnp2VmPCEw_nuABau-60ooUcxq27lVMceY6EVniR74VN1jCLuwCiL

Sobel, A. (2016). *Eight Ways to Improve Your Empathy | Andrew Sobel.* Andrewsobel.com. https://andrewsobel.com/eight-ways-to-improve-your-empathy/

Taylor, B. (n.d.). *How to Build Team Members Around You.* Small Business - Chron.com. Retrieved December 6, 2020, from https://smallbusiness.chron.com/build-team-members-around-17738.html

Young Entrepreneur Council. (2018, September 21). *10 Ways to Increase Your Emotional Intelligence.* Inc.com; Inc. https://

www.inc.com/young-entrepreneur-council/10-ways-to-increase-your-emotional-intelligence.html

Vistage Staff. (2020, January 6). *8 Qualities of the Best Executive Coaches | Vistage*. Vistage Research Center. https://www.vistage.com/research-center/business-leadership/20200106-8-qualities-of-the-best-executive-coaches/

What Is A Mindset Coach? Do I Need One? (2019, February 25). The Mindset Coach Academy. https://mindsetcoachacademy.com/what-is-a-mindset-coach-do-i-need-one/

webadmin. (2019, June 18). *Successful Business Leaders Who Had Coaches*. Knowted. https://knowted.co/successful-business-leaders-who-had-coaches/

Made in the USA
Middletown, DE
12 September 2021